Dedication

For my late father
to whom I dedicate this book

About the Series

The African Humanities Series is a partnership between the African Humanities Program (AHP) of the American Council of Learned Societies and academic publishers NISC (Pty) Ltd*. The Series covers topics in African histories, languages, literatures, philosophies, politics and cultures. Submissions are solicited from Fellows of the AHP, which is administered by the American Council of Learned Societies and financially supported by the Carnegie Corporation of New York.

The purpose of the AHP is to encourage and enable the production of new knowledge by Africans in the five countries designated by the Carnegie Corporation: Ghana, Nigeria, South Africa, Tanzania, and Uganda. AHP fellowships support one year's work free from teaching and other responsibilities to allow the Fellow to complete the project proposed. Eligibility for the fellowship in the five countries is by domicile, not nationality.

Book proposals are submitted to the AHP editorial board which manages the peer review process and selects manuscripts for publication by NISC. In some cases, the AHP board will commission a manuscript mentor to undertake substantive editing and to work with the author on refining the final manuscript.

The African Humanities Series aims to publish works of the highest quality that will foreground the best research being done by emerging scholars in the five Carnegie designated countries. The rigorous selection process before the fellowship award, as well as AHP editorial vetting of manuscripts, assures attention to quality. Books in the series are intended to speak to scholars in Africa as well as in other areas of the world.

The AHP is also committed to providing a copy of each publication in the series to university libraries in Africa.

*early titles in the series was published by Unisa Press, but the publishing rights to the entire series are now vested in NISC

Published in this series

White Narratives
The Depiction of Post-2000 Land Invasions in Zimbabwe

IRIKIDZAYI MANASE

AHP
Publications

NISC

Originally published in 2016 by Unisa Press, South Africa
under ISBN: 978-1-86888-825-2

This edition published in South Africa on behalf of the African Humanities
Program by NISC (Pty) Ltd, PO Box 377, Grahamstown, 6140, South Africa
www.nisc.co.za

NISC first edition, first impression 2019

ISBN: 978-1-920033-47-7 (print)
ISBN: 978-1-920033-48-4 (PDF)
ISBN: 978-1-920033-49-1 (ePub)

Book Designer: Lubabalo Qabaka
Project Editor: Tshegofatso Sehlodimela
Copyeditor: Kathryn-Jean Gibbs
Typesetting: Thea Bester-Swanepoel
Cover Image: Janaka Dharmasena, used under license from Shutterstock.com

Contents

Acknowledgements

I benefited from assistance and support from institutions, friends and colleagues in writing this book. I would like to especially acknowledge the American Council of Learned Societies (ACLS) African Humanities Program (AHP) for the Postdoctoral Fellowship grant that assisted me in writing this book. I also thank the ACLS AHP team for inviting me to a manuscript-writing workshop in Ghana, for their rigorous manuscript publishing competition and their awarding of funds to publish this book, and I would especially like thank Barbara van der Merwe, the AHP Secretariat at the Johannesburg office, for all the logistical support, encouragement and quick responses to my emails.

A number of individuals played an important role in the writing of this book. I thank my brother-in-law, Edwin Mungadzi, for giving me Cathy Buckle's memoirs in 2003; this opened my eyes to the growth of the body of white narratives about the post-2000 land invasions. A number of colleagues read the manuscript and offered valuable criticism. I want to thank Robert Muponde in particular for his insightful criticism. I also thank Michael Wessels, Francis Garaba, Terrence Musanga and Tendai Mupanduki for their assistance in different ways as well as encouraging me to soldier on with the writing of the book. My special thanks to Wendy Willems and Rory Pilossof for sharing some of their work which added value to my research and writing.

Finally, I would like to thank my wife and children for the support they gave me during the period of researching and writing this book.

Introduction
Imaginaries of Land and Belonging

In this book I draw on Alexander's (2007:183) view which links land with the construction of identities, the formation of classes and the crafting of artistic principles and spiritual meanings. Through a literary analysis of selected memoirs, fictional and non-fictional texts I describe the nature and effects of the post-2000 Zimbabwe land invasions, referred to as the 'fast track land reform programme' by the Zimbabwe government. The book examines the diverse nature of the narratives and perceptions about land, belonging and the way in which the Zimbabwe government influenced the politics of identities through a revision of identification and race categories (Brubaker and Cooper 2000) during this turbulent post-2000 period. It also considers issues about white narratives on land and belonging, well aware of the existence of a huge body of conflicting studies and public perceptions on the causes, justification and impact of the land invasions and the subsequent fast track land reform programme in Zimbabwe. This book therefore seeks to answer a number of questions such as: Why was there a flurry of white Zimbabwean narratives about land? How are the land invasions represented in these white narratives? How are perceptions about belonging treated in these texts? What are the solutions offered to the contestations for land and belonging in these white narratives?

What became clear in my research for this book was that ownership of and perceptions about land have been contested in the Zimbabwean social imaginary from the pre-colonial to the post-independence eras. Discourses about the landscape are linked with European imperialism (Mitchell 1994), and with Zimbabwe's pre-colonial and colonial history as outlined by Mackenzie (1988), replete with European hunters' and concession seekers' exploitation of the Mashonaland and Matabeleland regions' natural resources, which led to the subsequent control of parts of both regions by the imperialist British South Africa Company (BSAC). Other highlights of the contestations relate to the post-1900s BSAC's enactment of land ordinances that expropriated vast tracts of land from the indigenous African societies and turned it into Company and Crown land and the associated establishment of white settlements, commercial farms and mining centres at the expense of the original African owners of these lands who were displaced, as evidenced by the relocations of the Ndebele from the Bulawayo area to Gwai and Shangani (Alexander, McGregor and Ranger 2000). The indigenous peoples were thus removed from their land and denied access to other natural resources. The contestations also resulted from the colonised Zimbabweans' subversion of the dominance of the BSAC rule as noted in the 1893 Anglo-Ndebele War and the 1896–1897 Ndebele-Shona Uprisings. Later subversion is witnessed in the 1970s black nationalist resistance to white Rhodesian settler rule (Alexander et al 2000; Ranger 2000).

Central to these various conflicts are opposing perceptions about belonging, access, ownership and usage of land and other available natural resources. What is also critical here is the way black and indigenous perceptions about conservation conflicted with those of the BSAC and later Rhodesian settler perceptions. The BSAC and Rhodesian settler perceptions were located in British and imperial discourses based on European scientific and geographic values, while the Ndebele and Shona based their perceptions on land and conservation on utilitarian, social and religious values. This impacted on the social imaginary and control of the land. The BSAC and later Rhodesian settlers, on the one hand entrenched their economic and political control over the land from 1910 to the 1960s, through the introduction of land division laws, such as the 1930 Land Apportionment Act and the Land Husbandry Act of 1951 which displaced the colonised Africans from land designated for white commercial farming and human settlements, and controlled tenure on African villages and settlements. The colonised African communities, on the other hand, began to organise politically, especially from the 1950s onwards until their engagement in radical anti-colonial military activism directed against Rhodesian colonial rule in the 1970s. The unfair distribution of land and the general displeasure at the dehumanisation and brutality associated with colonial oppression were the major driving forces in the anti-colonial resistance which culminated in the attainment of national independence in 1980.

The contestations over land have, however, continued to plague Zimbabwe's social and political imaginary. The land imbalances inherited from the imperial BSAC and settler Rhodesian eras that disadvantaged the indigenous Ndebele and Shona communities, were not fully corrected by the nationalist Zimbabwe African National Union Patriotic Front (Zanu-PF) government which succeeded the colonial Rhodesian government in 1980. The various land reform programmes that were introduced by the Zanu-PF government from 1980 to the late 1990s did not change the colonially inherited land distribution patterns and social memories about belonging and access to the land. As a result, tensions and anxieties continued to fester among ordinary black Zimbabweans. The post-2000 land invasions and their pursuit of a radical change to the definition of historical memory and ownership of land, under the guise of an anti-Euro-American imperialism stance, can therefore, to some extent, be traced to the Zanu-PF government's failure to redistribute land after 1980.

However, the land invasions have been associated with violence, the general destabilisation of farming activities and the displacement of white farmers and their black farmworkers. The controversies and contestations experienced in Zimbabwe during the height of the land invasions in Zimbabwe polarised the country and its public sectors. This is aptly discussed by Willems (2004a; 2004b) in her examination of the conflicting representations of the invasions in the media and in Pilossof's (2012) historical study of the discourses related to white Zimbabwean farmer experiences during the colonial era and in the post-independence era, especially during the post-2000 era. On an interesting note, Kalaora's (2011) anthropological study on the white Zimbabwean farmer experiences during the post-2000 period reveal further divisions within the white community, as they considered some of the survivalist strategies, where a farmer would work with a local black Zimbabwean settler or politician in order to stay on the land, something frowned upon by some whites who had lost their land and were not willing to work with the new black settlers. It should be emphasised, though, that the Zanu-PF government launched a media, cultural and ideological campaign that sought to justify land invasions and manipulate the ordinary Zimbabweans' perceptions about the land, belonging and racial categories (Chuma 2004; Thram 2006). Hammar and Raftopoulos (2003) consider this strategy as resulting in the constitution of a post-2000 imaginary of land that is monolithic and singular as it valorised the ideological and selective historical interpretation propounded by the Zanu-PF party.

Nevertheless, what is significant for this book is that the post-2000 period witnessed a fervent production of literary and cultural narratives that describe experiences and imaginings about the land invasions. My book examines past and present historical, ideological, social and spatial divisions in the definition of the experiences, conflicts and ambiguities arising from the land invasions, as depicted in the selected fictional, non-fictional texts and memoirs written by the white commercial farmers and other white writers with connections either to the land or some of the displaced farmers. While acknowledging the contribution of other historical studies, such as Pilossof's (2012) seminal text on Zimbabwean white farmer experiences, my book seeks to add to this body of studies a dimension which draws on a sustained literary analysis of some of the white narratives about the invasions and the fast track land reform programme.

The book is thus arranged as follows: the first chapter introduces the study. The second chapter considers the fact that the texts are varied in genre and thus elicit an interdisciplinary paradigm of enquiry. Post-colonial concerns about imperialism, colonial discourses and the contestations over history and social memory – postulated by Ashcroft (1994) and Chennells (1999) – are therefore considered. Ideas proffered by scholars including Mackenzie (1988), Ranger (1999 a; 1999b; 2000; 2005), Kalaora (2011), Pilossof (2012) and Hartnack (2014) that relate to the centrality of history in the contestations over the control and definition of land and its aesthetics in Rhodesia and Zimbabwe are reviewed. Also evaluated is Chennells' (1995) insightful study of the nature of Rhodesian fiction and its representation of the settler-colonialist discourses about the land. This is juxtaposed with an appraisal of the social and literary history of Zimbabwe, especially that which treats the theme of land in black Zimbabwean literature as discussed by Veit-Wild (1993). The rise to eminence of the 'Rhodesian chronotope' – an imperialist definition of the land that limited the movements of the inferior and colonised 'other' into and out of the white areas, which re-emerges in the post-2000 period under the ideological control of the Zanu-PF government (Primorac 2006) is also taken into consideration in this chapter.

Furthermore, the significance of theoretical perspectives on life narratives, the redemptive story and ecocriticism is considered in Chapter 2. Life narratives involve a narrator's retelling of events, which are mostly negative, and encountered in the past in an effort to compel them to make narrative sense, find meaning in the suffering and in the process move on with their lives (McAdams 2008:253–254). As such, the role of concepts about life stories in enabling us as readers to determine personal and societal transformation resulting from the crises encountered by white commercial farmers and families is discussed. This will assist in evaluating the experiences of the Rogers family in Chapter 6. In addition, theoretical concepts drawing on post-colonial ecocriticism are reviewed. Considered here is the nexus between ecology and imperialism, racism and the environment, and competing discourses between the West and the South on notions about development (Huggan and Tiffin 2010) in the examination of the impact of the land invasions on human-animal relations, as depicted in Buckle's text examined in Chapter 7.

Chapter 3 examines Catherine Buckle's memoirs *African Tears: The Zimbabwean Land Invasions* (2000) and *Beyond Tears: Zimbabwe's Tragedy* (2003). Both memoirs document the author's personal experiences during and after the invasion of her farm, Stow Farm, which she and her husband had bought a few years before. Alexander's (2007) postulations about land and how it is dialectically linked to the constitution of identity and the mapping of historical and social imaginaries are used as a starting point for the development of an analytical yarn seeking to examine the nature and effect of the invasions on the writer's social and economic well-being. Buckle's creative agency, noted in her factual depiction of violence and the ultimate employment of multiple styles and an activist tone in her narrative style, is discussed. The writer's subversion of the ruling party's black nationalist ideological rhetoric, which was used by its supporters to justify the land invasions, is examined under post-colonial perspectives, such as Fanon's (1964) ideas on the role of violence in the colonial and anti-colonial project. Other post-colonial notions focussing on identity formation and displacement are considered. The chapter concludes with an evaluation of the significance of both texts in illustrating Buckle's role in expanding Zimbabwe's literary form.

Chapter 4 examines representations of the effects of the land invasions on the Bourke siblings as depicted in Graham Lang's *Place of Birth* (2006). The chapter scrutinises Vaughn Bourke (a Rhodesian-born migrant permanently resident in Australia) and his siblings' experiences during the period of the invasions. The major events here are the family reunion in Bulawayo and their journey back to their besieged farm outside Bulawayo to exhume their ancestors' remains so that they can rebury them at a nearby farming town's church cemetery. Post-colonial notions of place and dislocation (Macgregor 2006; Ashcroft et al 1995) are teased out as the Bourkes reveal the different locations that they are coming from and how the land invasions have displaced them from the personal memories and ties to the family farm that had been passed from one generation to the next since the 1890s. The role of the landscape and space in the constitution of identities and in imprinting personal histories is considered and juxtaposed to the Zimbabwean state's grand narrative about the land that overshadowed all personal histories and narratives about the land.

Chapter 5 examines Christina Lamb's *House of Stone: The True Story of a Family Divided in War-Torn Zimbabwe* (2006). The reportage-based text is set during the height of the post-2000 land invasions and describes the experiences of a white commercial farmer, David Hough, and his family, and their relations with their black Zimbabwean domestic worker, Aquinata. It incorporates the autobiographical genre and employs flashbacks to inscribe the different life experiences undergone by both chief protagonists from their early childhood in the 1970s through to their adult lives in the 1980s and their current experiences on the farm during the post-2000 land invasions. The text draws on the country's past and present history to depict its significance in inscribing the existence of divided worlds in colonial and post-colonial Zimbabwe and their impact in shaping the imaginings about the land invasions. The chapter is informed by Noyes' (1992) and Fanon's (1963) discussions on the nature and impact of the colonial spatial divisions in the experiences of the colonised and their construction of identities. Hence, I analyse the relevance of the author's narrative point of view – that colonially established social divisions contribute to the constitution of multiple narratives about the land and the different perceptions of Zimbabwe's social and political history which are at stake in the mapping of the land invasions and contestations over belonging.

Chapter 6 examines the contribution of Douglas Rogers' memoir, *The Last Resort: A Memoir of Zimbabwe* (2009), to the portrayal of the impact of the land invasions on both the way the affected white farmers perceived and understood themselves and their parent-child relations. The writer describes both his parents' and his own story during the post-2000 land invasions. The personal narrative genre is invoked in this memoir as the author describes his parents' experiences at their farm and tourist lodge, Drifters, outside Mutare, struggling to prevent their eviction and loss of the property to war veterans and supporters of the Zanu-PF party. The chapter draws on concepts about life narratives and the redemptive story. This is where the narrator is encouraged to narrate about negative events encountered in the past in an effort to compel them to make narrative sense, find meaning in the suffering and in the process move on with their lives (McAdams 2008:253–254). As such, the chapter considers the role of life stories in enabling us as readers to determine the transformative personalities and senses of the self that were constructed by some white commercial farmers and families during the period. This will assist in the evaluation of the experiences of the Rogers family and determine the possible solutions to this crisis, especially by evaluating the survival strategies, redemptive selves and new relationships and connectedness constituted during the land-invasion crisis.

Chapter 7 examines Catherine Buckle's *Innocent Victims: Rescuing the Stranded Animals of Zimbabwe's Farm Invasions* (2009) which is based on representations of the diarised experiences of Meryl Harrison, a white Zimbabwean Society for the Prevention of Cruelty to Animals (SPCA) inspector and animal rights activist, between July 2000 and December 2004. It considers the impact of the post-2000 land invasions on human-animal interactions and ecology at the affected farms, as well as the formation of Meryl Harrison's activism and experiences as she travelled around Zimbabwe to rescue the stranded animals. The chapter considers, to a great extent, Huggan and Tiffin's (2010:4–17) argument that there is the need to recognise that the environment and animals have contributed greatly to the development of societies and human lives; and that in cases where a given people enjoy a limited measure of access to social and cultural spheres of the environment, post-colonial ecocriticism seeks to speak against such dominance, in the form of an environmentally located advocacy. The chapter, thus, argues that the ecological crisis and victimisation of farm and wild animals witnessed by Meryl disrupt notions of belonging and ultimately emblematise the contradictions associated with the post-colonial trajectories of Zimbabwe since 2000; for one would have expected a remapping of access and belonging to the land that seeks to create and maintain a balance between humans, animals and environment.

Chapter 8 sums up the issues that dominate the various representations of the post-2000 land invasions and how this impacts on the contemporary post-colonial conditions in Zimbabwe. A brief discussion on the strands about land that are beyond the scope of this study, is made as a way of unpacking the way the imaginaries about land have continued to be contentious and hence in need of further research in Zimbabwean literary and cultural studies.

An interdisciplinary approach that incorporates perspectives from post-colonial studies, the media, history, and landscape and conservation ideas, will be used in this study. The intention is to examine how themes such as belonging and 'unbelonging', rights to the land, aesthetics on the landscape, and memory and the land are treated. The main focus is to evaluate whether the existing myths and discourses on the land are being extended or new ones created as a result of the recent narratives and texts on the land in Zimbabwe. Hence, the represented multi-layered social and political contestations between white commercial farmers and the state, blacks and whites, the opposition and the ruling party, and Zimbabwe and the international community are considered within the field of literary studies and other theoretical perspectives from history, landscape and conservation studies.

The issue of the land and land redistribution in Zimbabwe has been and continues to be topical in the media and political discussions. A number of studies from the field of history, anthropology and other social sciences have been produced. These analyse the experiences of white Zimbabwean farmers and their establishment of belonging in settler Rhodesia and independent Zimbabwe as noted in Hughes (2010) and Pilossof (2012), and others, such as Hanlon, Manjengwa and Smart (2013), examine the experiences and impact of the black farmers who benefited from the fast track land reform programme in the Zimbabwean economy. Yet, there is a lack of an in-depth literary study of the representation of the land from the critical period of 2000 to 2010 – by 2009 the general rhetoric was that the fast track land reform programme had come to an end, owing to the formation of the Government of National Unity between the Zanu-PF and MDC. In fact, Pilossof (2012) in his introduction to the historical study on white Zimbabwean farmer experiences acknowledges that there is a lack of critical studies on this subject and so my book is an attempt at filling this gap from a literary perspective. This is therefore a qualitative study that incorporates post-colonial, cultural, historical and landscape theories via a literary survey of selected fictional and non-fictional texts, focusing on experiences based on the land in post-2000 Zimbabwe.

The Post-2000 Zimbabwe Crisis and the Writings about the Land

The major question about literature in post-independence Zimbabwe is why there is a significant increase in the production of literary works by white writers after 2000. Although there had been a long tradition and huge output of writings by white Rhodesian authors prior to independence, as noted in Chennells's (1982) seminal thesis, the period after 1980 witnessed a decrease in the production of literary works from white Zimbabweans with the situation only improving with a surge of writing in the post-2000 era. The answer to the question is partly linked to the historical events leading to the crisis conditions after 2000 which act as an impetus to the white narratives under study in this book.

The post-2000 period in Zimbabwe is generally characterised by severe social, political and economic instability. This instability can be linked to the Zanu-PF's reaction to the formation of a formidable opposition political party, the Movement for Democratic Change (MDC) in 1999 and its collaboration with civic organisations, such as the National Constitution Assembly (NCA) the Zimbabwe Crisis Coalition (ZCC) and Women of Zimbabwe Arise (WOZA) in the campaign for better democratic conditions in the country. The opposition and civic organisation groups campaigned for people-driven constitutional reforms and wider participation of all Zimbabweans, irrespective of race, ethnicity or political affiliation, in the implementation and exercise of various personal, intellectual and other freedoms. Meanwhile, the former nationalist liberation movement and ruling party, the Zimbabwe African National Union Patriotic Front (Zanu-PF) had dominated Zimbabwe since 1980. From the late 1990s its governance of Zimbabwe has been characterised by the limitation of citizens' freedoms and pronounced post-colonial tyranny. The major highlights of the Zanu-PF governance from 1980 to 2000 include the state-sponsored violent suppression of military insurgency, termed the 'dissidents' era', in the Matabeleland province and the resultant annihilation of people from the region known popularly as the 'Gukurahundi massacres'. The period also witnessed the state's dabbling with the World Bank and the International Monetary Fund's (IMF) economic structural reforms. As a result, the 1990s witnessed the government moving away from providing subsidies in public sectors such as education and health, and the opening up of the economy to foreign competition, under the IMF-prescribed ethos of a liberalised economy.

The 1990s economic reforms resulted in several local companies closing, retrenchments and a rise in the cost of living. The working class and other ordinary Zimbabweans bore the brunt of these social, political and economic hardships to the extent that the Zimbabwe Congress of Trade Unions (ZCTU), with Morgan Tsvangirai as the Secretary General, began to organise protests against the government and called for measures that would ameliorate the citizens' conditions. The late 1990s were thus marked by a fervent anti-state agency that was led by the ZCTU, tertiary student movements and some church and civic organisations. This resulted in the formation of the MDC which became a formidable political opposition that had the support of black and white urban residents, especially from the middle and working classes and those from various civic organisations as well as the white commercial farming sector. One of the issues at stake was the need to open up the political space by introducing political reform, beginning with constitutional reforms.

The land, which had become a topical issue in Zimbabwean politics after 1990, was also under much debate and Zimbabwean whites felt threatened by the state's land designation and land reform proposals. The subsequent February 2000 constitutional referendum, held after contested national consultations, resulted in the people's rejection of the Zanu-PF-engineered draft constitution. This signalled the beginning of a new era in national politics, as the Zanu-PF party faced its first major challenge since Zimbabwe attained its independence in 1980. In reaction to the threat of opposition, former war of liberation veterans and other Zanu-PF supporters then went on to occupy selected white-owned commercial farms in February 2000, marking the beginning of a series of systematic land invasions in Zimbabwe plunging the country into a huge social, economic and political crisis, as outlined by Hammar and Raftopoulos (2003), Hill (2003) and Nyamunda (2014).

Between 2000 and 2008 we continued to witness profound contestations between the ruling party Zanu-PF and the opposition MDC over the control of national political spaces. The period is also characterised by the occurrence of invasions and occupations of commercial farms that were under the control of white Zimbabweans as well as those owned by black Zimbabweans sympathetic to the opposition. The invasions were carried out in retaliation against the white commercial farmers' open support and involvement in the opposition MDC structures which fought against the government-proposed national constitutional reforms in 2000 and sought to unseat Zanu-PF from the national political space.

The land invasions, it must be noted, were also related to Britain's New Labour Party announcement in 1997 that it bore no responsibility for their country's past colonial injustices. As a result, Zimbabwe's claim for financial aid for the land reforms was not supported by the Labour Party government. Phimister (2005:121–123) outlines further that the New Labour's policy shift, was compounded by its introduction of the concept of 'liberal imperialism', where Britain announced it would fight all failed states in the world in order to restore order and at the same time ally with the United States of America in its global anti-terrorism campaign after the 11 September 2001 terrorist attacks. This allowed the Zanu-PF government to craft an anti-imperialism grand narrative as it was being criticised by Britain, America and other Western countries for not respecting property rights, the rule of law and for being intolerant to opposition. The grand narrative is described by Primorac (2007:435) as 'Zimbabwe's state fiction' that was constructed after 2000 when the state began interfering in the social and political trajectories of the nation. This narrative mapped the MDC, civic organisations and white commercial farmers as working in collaboration with the British to effect regime change and subsequently re-colonise Zimbabwe. As a result, the country began to witness the persecution of opposition and civic activists of all races; the censorship of the country's media; severe police and military control of citizens' movement and their social and private spaces; and the punitive and overzealous inspection of retail, transport and financial service entities carried out by the government price-monitoring officers as the country's social, political economic sectors spiralled downwards after 2000.

The Zanu-PF government and its repressive agents who included the former war of liberation fighters and the youth militia introduced an aggressive campaign against the opposition and other civic organisations during different parliamentary and presidential elections, especially the 2000, 2002 and 2005 elections. The land was defined as a national resource, belonging to black Zimbabweans, which had to be liberated from white farmers and at the same time guarded jealously against any possible imperialist take over by Britain, America and its local supporters represented by the MDC. Thus, the invasions were defined as part of the final war seeking to liberate land and other national resources from white and foreign control. Furthermore, Zimbabwean elections were fought over the land, with the Zanu-PF coming up with narratives and campaign slogans such as, 'The land is the economy and the economy is the land', during the 2002 elections.

The land issue continued to dominate the political discourse of Zimbabwe throughout the period 2000 to 2008. State media, which was aligned to the Zanu-PF, and the independent media, which supported the MDC and other civic groups, published contesting views about the land reforms during the period under study (Willems 2004a). The state's mapping of the land invasions had changed over the years, from '*jambanja*' which implied the invasion and forced eviction of white farmers from their land during the first two years, to the sanitised 'fast track land reform programme'. From around 2002 onwards, the intrusions into and occupation of the white commercial farms were now defined as a process that would result in a quicker redistribution of land among ordinary Zimbabweans, who had been dispossessed historically. Nevertheless, as noted by Pilossof (2008:207), Zanu-PF still drew on the 'land card' to drum up support in the 2008 presidential elections, despite the declaration that the fast track land reform objectives had been accomplished by about 2007. This, therefore, shows the centrality of the land issue in the politics and social imaginary of the twenty-first century Zimbabwean post-colonial condition.

The invasions and the subsequent fast track land reform programme impacted heavily on the different sectors of the country. Perceptions of the impact of land invasions on the other sectors were contested. On the one hand, the Zanu-PF's perception was emblematised by the 2002 election slogan, 'The land is the economy and the economy is the land', which placed the ownership of the land, through the process of land occupations and the fast track land distribution, as central to Zimbabwe's economic prosperity and independence from imperial domination. On the other hand, the occupation of farms and their redistribution, which were mostly characterised by violence and the non-provision of compensation to the former farm owners, were perceived in the business sector and in the West as a major violation of one of the key elements of business: the respect for property rights. This violation of property rights led to the creation of uncertainty in other areas of business. Pilossof (2008:272–273) reviews the thought productions related to this strand that were produced by Richardson in *The Collapse of Zimbabwe in the Wake of the 2000–2003 Land Reforms* and sums them up as narrow and reductionist:

> Richardson blames the ruin of Zimbabwe squarely on the government's disregard for property right laws. [...] This narrow and reductionist reading of the Zimbabwean situation has its limited merits, but more interestingly shows that this type of ahistorical reading of an economic implosion has its limitations. Wholesale and widespread respect for property rights is not applicable to every situation, especially when the situation involves a colonial legacy that has not been adequately dealt with or resolved.

Pilossof's views indicate that the impact of the post-2000 land invasions and the causes of the Zimbabwe crisis are complex and need to be examined from the specific historical developments in Zimbabwe in addition to the country's relations with Britain and other Western powers.

Nevertheless, the relational linkages between the land invasions and the destabilisation of the agricultural sector with the subsequent collapse of other economic sectors, such as the manufacturing, retail and financial services sectors, and the decline of local government and other social services proves otherwise. It is clear that the way the ruling Zanu-PF government handled the historically justified need to redistribute land to the majority of land-hungry Zimbabweans created fertile ground for the gradual economic decline between 2000 and 2004. The economic decline degenerated to exponential inflationary levels and the establishment of a shortage economy from 2005 onwards.

The impact of the land invasions and the miserable conditions that ordinary Zimbabweans endured is best represented in Tagwira's (2007) *Uncertainty of Hope*, where the novelist portrays urban residents, made up of an array of characters that include university students and a beneficiary of the land reform, encounter everyday life experiences that are characterised by poverty, a shortage of basic commodities and declining health and other public services. In addition, the decline of the general populace's living conditions compelled some Zimbabweans to migrate to neighbouring countries in the region and major Western countries such as the United Kingdom, the United States of America, Canada and Australia. Chikwava's *Harare North* (2009) is one fictional text that treats the nexus between the post-2000 Zimbabwe crisis and migration to metropolitan cities such as London. More importantly, whites from all walks of life produced writings in the form of memoirs, non-fictional and fictional works, which described their experiences on the land, their displacement from the farms and other experiences related to perceptions about land, views on their positions in the nation and on belonging and the ensuing ecological crisis. As a result, the post-2000 land invasions were synonymous with crisis conditions, but acted as a prompt to various literary productions, especially the white narratives, which are the subject of this book.

This book acknowledges that the Zimbabwean state and its citizens have been severely affected by the social, political and economic crisis that began in 2000. However, it focuses on the impact of the crisis within a particular sector of Zimbabwean society, namely the commercial farmers, their families and their workers, as portrayed in selected white imaginings and representations of the post-2000 land invasions. This study examines white writings that describe the experiences, thoughts, memories and contestations over land in post-2000 Zimbabwe. The experiences and concerns depicted in some of the texts cover wide issues that include the personal and private, and those related to national identity, where race, history and ideology are interrogated. Concerns about human-animal relations, environmental conservation and landscape aesthetics are also unpacked owing to the contestations based on land use and conservationist histories between the commercial farmers and those who lived on or held memories of the disputed land. In addition, it examines conflicting narratives, where personal and family histories are undermined by an overarching nationalist narrative that justifies the land appropriations and the formation of new forms of writing and discourse that test established theories and conventions of creative writing and cultural productions.

History: The Mapping of Land-Use Patterns and the Construction of Perceptions about Land

An apt entry point into a review of the theoretical ideas informing this study is a consideration of the role of history in shaping ownership and land-use patterns – termed 'aesthetic perceptions of the environment' by

Ranger (2000:53) – whose different readings are outlined by Mitchell (1994:5) as including the thesis that 'landscape is a particular historical formation associated with European imperialism'. Also considered is the role of history in the ideological contestations as well as the anti-colonial struggle in determining the literary and cultural imaginings of the land. It should be underscored that there are different histories, ranging from the colonial, literary and personal to national histories that are interwoven with contestations over the land in Zimbabwe. Ranger's (2005:242) view that 'history is at the centre of politics in Zimbabwe far more than any other southern African country' is significant here. Furthermore, history is also central in the different aspects related to the representations of the land in Zimbabwe as depicted in the literary and cultural texts under focus in this study. These histories and the representations of the land are unstable, multiple and constantly subverting the dominant forces, be they British imperialism or settler Rhodesian rule, to draw on intimations made by Chennells (1999:116) in his postulations on post-colonial theory and African literature.

The first strand in the examination of history and its role in shaping land-use patterns, ownership and perceptions of land in Zimbabwe is related to the European hunters' and the BSAC's intrusion into Matabeleland and Mashonaland and the subsequent establishment of the BSAC and Rhodesian settler colonialism. The intrusion into both pre-colonial Matabeleland and Mashonaland by European hunters, adventurers, explorers and missionaries resulted in the huge exploitation of the regions' game, such as elephant, rhinoceros, lion, buffalo and hippopotamus for their horns, hides and trophies that were sold at various trading ports along the southern African coastline (Mackenzie 1988). These activities mapped the pre-colonial Zimbabwean landscape as a space available for European conquest and exploitation, thus fitting into one of Mitchell's (1994:5) theses on the landscape and power where he juxtaposes the landscape with imperialism. These moments of contact, viewed as indicative of the beginning of post-colonialism (Ashcroft 1994:33–34; Chennells 1999:110), marked the commencement of the imperial reconfiguration of the Zimbabwean land and landscape into spaces meant for the West's domination and consumption, as happened elsewhere on the African continent and in some parts of Asia, Australia, New Zealand and the Americas.

In fact, the hunters and adventurers expanded the frontiers of European power into central Africa. European influence expanded every time the European hunters and adventurers moved from the lower parts of southern Africa into the interior in search of rich hunting grounds as the game rapidly depleted. This expansion acted as a stepping stone towards cultural and political domination as some of the figures, such as Thomas Morgan and David Livingstone, engaged in both hunting and the spread of Christian missionary stations in Central Africa (Mackenzie 1988:85–146). The conflict between Europeans and Africans in pre-colonial Zimbabwe over natural resources such as the land and over perceptions of their exploitation and ownership were thus established in Zimbabwe. The subsequent intrusion into Mashonaland in 1890 and the 1893 Anglo-Ndebele War resulted in the BSAC establishing colonial settlements seeking to exploit the land, mainly for agriculture and mining and other industries. It enhanced the Euro-African divisions concerning perceptions of ownership of the land. The European reconfiguration of the landscape involved the expropriation of land from the Ndebele and the Shona, often through war, such as the 1893 and 1896 wars, and coercive means as the Company's land expropriation laws were implemented (Ranger 1999b and 2000). Vast tracts of land were cordoned off and turned into private spaces for white settler occupation and this created clashes based on culture (European/African), race (white/black), land use patterns (private and commercial/communal) and historical perspectives (the colonial historiography of empty landscapes/the nationalist discourse that the land belongs to the Africans).

The Africans also lost land under violent circumstances, especially during the post-1897 period as they were forcibly moved to designated African reserves, the first of which were the inhospitable and disease-ridden areas of Gwai and Shangani in Matabeleland. This process continued into the 1950s under the notorious 1930 Land Apportionment Act and other restrictive agrarian laws as succinctly discussed by Alexander, MacGregor and Ranger (2000) in their study of the history of the Gwai-Shangani area in Matabeleland. The European intrusion and settler appropriation of land therefore went hand in hand with the establishment of political domination over Zimbabwe. It also established the divisions and anxieties between the colonial subjects and the coloniser. This positioned the land at the centre of all future conflicts, such as the social and political clashes between the Rhodesian settlers and the African colonial subjects, the war of liberation and the conflict between contemporary white commercial farmers and the nationalist Zanu-PF government as will be discussed later.

It is also pertinent that I underscore, from the outset, the significance of the impact of European and African perceptions of the landscape and conservation in this book. As already noted, the Europeans' intrusion into pre-colonial Matabeleland and Mashonaland resulted in a heavy exploitation of the regions' natural resources, a trend that continued well into the pioneer and Rhodesian settler farmers' consolidation of their hold on the colony. The depletion of wild game went hand in hand with the process of imperial expansion (Mackenzie 1988:85–146) and the colonialists' inscription of their power on the colonial landscape continued in the form of hunting and the harvesting of wood from the forests for the European mines and settlements. This indicates the Europeans' power over the land, their colonial processes of capitalist accumulation and settler entrenchment in the colony, which resulted in the marginalisation of the local Africans.

Nevertheless, the imperial project, as enshrined in the vision of Cecil John Rhodes and some environmentally conscious company and settler administrators, noted the need to conserve the colonial Zimbabwean landscape (Ranger 1999b:56–66). This marked the beginning of another strand in the historiography of the country and discourses about the landscape where European and African perceptions about how to conserve nature in colonial Rhodesia were at odds with each other.

Ranger's (1999b) in-depth historical study of the culture and nature of the Matopos Hills shows the struggle over the control and interpretations of the hills' cultural and landscape symbolism. The conflict between the white settler administrators and farmers, on the one hand, and the Banyubi groups of people, as well as other Ndebele and Kalanga people who lived and hunted on the lands around the hills and performed religious and cultural ceremonies to venerate the Mwari cult, on the other hand, was often marked by violence. This is evidenced by the 1893 Anglo-Ndebele War and the 1896–97 Ndebele-Shona Uprising, which ended with intense battles around the hills and by the subsequent truces and settlements that were agreed on at the Matopos as noted by Ranger (1999b:27–32). It is clear that the hills, where the Mwari cult provided guidance on matters of religion, agriculture (rain-making) and war to both the Ndebele and Shona people, constituted the landscape in the African nationalist and cultural resistance against BSAC and white settler domination. This explains why Rhodes chose to be buried in the Matopos Hills, which was a means to appropriate the land considered sacred by the Africans and thus inscribe his colonial and cultural authority on the landscape too. Rhodes' burial was interpreted by the colonial writers as 'reshaping the landscape and triumphing over the African spirit guardians of the hills' (Ranger 1999b:31). The hills thus became a site of cultural contestations and its significance is noted in its incorporation into the nationalist discourse during the 1970s war of liberation and in the post-independence era.

The conflict that ensued between the settler agricultural and conservation scientists and the African community over the landscape of the Matopos should be highlighted. This conflict typifies the opposing perceptions on how to use and conserve the landscape. The conflict also greatly influences the contradictory discourses and literary imaginings of the land that are reflected in some of the texts under study in this book. Ranger (1999b:56–66) outlines Rhodes' vision, which sought to preserve the beautiful landscape around the Matopos for the benefit of the future and how this led to the birth of colonial conservationist discourses, some of which stereotyped the African communities as lacking scientifically appropriate and ecologically friendly practices. This, as noted by Ranger (2000:55), created a conflict over the environment between the colonial authorities and the colonised. The colonial administrators, agriculturalists and conservationists fervently pursued a conservationist and modernising project, as described by Bunn (1996) in his study of the establishment of game reserves in South Africa. A huge part of the Matopos would be transformed into a National Park and some into white settler commercial farms that supported scientifically based agricultural practices, unlike the practises engaged in by Africans which were seen to involve overgrazing, stream-bank agriculture and the clearing of natural forests to the detriment of indigenous trees, flowers and wild game (Ranger 1999b:56–66). The colonial administrators inscribed themselves on the colonial landscape as the protectors of the natural environment and as authoritative figures drawing on scientific principles, as noted in the various agricultural research stations that were established around the regions of the colony. The perceptions, typical of colonial discourses, mapped the Europeans as holders of superior ideals on matters such as civilisation and conservation, while Africans were regarded as uncivilised, ignorant and indifferent to the environment.

This is quite ironic, considering that, as already pointed in reference to Mackenzie's (1988) examination of European hunting and adventurers in central and southern Africa, the pre-colonial and the early colonial era's European intrusion into the region was characterised by the plunder of African natural resources. More so, white settlers' and the various Native Commissioners' violent and indiscriminate implementation of programmes that displaced Africans from the Crown Land and the land designated for white settlers and national parks resulted in the degradation of uninhabited and sparsely peopled lands that had huge indigenous tree forests, wild game and virgin soils. The Gusu forests in the Gwai-Shangani region, for example, were depleted as the new African settlers cleared the land to settle and till the lands and they subsequently became overcrowded (Alexander, MacGregor and Ranger 2000:45–60). Nevertheless, Ranger (1999b:23–25) points out that the Africans had a special cultural and religious relationship with the Matopos which guided their interaction with the landscape and thus ensured that it remained sacred and hence conserved.

However, the land invasions after 2000 have invoked a shift from Ranger's (2000) ideas on the landscape and ecology in Zimbabwe. The invasions have had lasting effects on the farms' wild and domestic animals, and have been associated with the rise of poaching in the country's conservancies, as described in Buckle's (2009) storying of Meryl Harrison's experiences as an animal protection officer during the period under focus, which is discussed in Chapter 7. We are compelled to evaluate the impact of the land invasions on human-animal relations and the ecology, drawing on Huggan and Tiffin's (2010:4–17) views about ecological imperialism, racism and the environment and conflicting ideas on what development is in Western and African discourses, in the consideration of new discourses and practices introduced on the occupied farms.

Zimbabwean history is indeed punctuated with conflicts over perceptions of the interpretation and protection of the landscape, owing to new settler divisions of the land based on race and power. Here, the conflict mirrors the role played by differences in culture and knowledge bases, where the dominant impose their values on the dominated. During the colonial era the white settlers valorised their European perceptions and scientific ideas about the environment and their inscriptions on the colonial landscape. Then later on, as reflected in the early twenty-first century Zimbabwean conditions, the nationalist Zanu-PF government and their supporters used values enshrined in the nationalist and anti-imperialist ideology as justifications for land seizures and the introduction of their land-use patterns. This often provoked horror and displaced psyches among the white commercial farmers and other white Zimbabweans as portrayed in some of the texts studied in this book.

Another important aspect, related to the intersection between history and the land, and the writings about the land, focuses on the centrality of the land in the nationalist resistance and the war of liberation in the 1970s. This historiography is fundamental in the creation of the anti-colonial and resistant nationalist discourses and agency that are witnessed from 1900 until the achievement of national independence in 1980. The history of Zimbabwe, as noted by, among other scholars, Palmer (1977), Ranger (1999b; 2000; 2005), Primorac (2006) and Alexander, MacGregor and Ranger (2000) is littered with conflicts over the land, from the moment the BSAC realised that there was a low mineral base in Mashonaland and turned their mission into that of creating a white settler agricultural colony in the 1900s which lasted until Zimbabwe gained independence in 1980.

The significance of land in the nationalist discourse, memory and national identity of Zimbabwe is further revealed in the land reforms implemented during the early post-independence period. The failure of these reforms further complicated the country's post-colonial history as the land issue again rose into prominence in the post-2000 political space. This forced the Zanu-PF led government and its supporters to invade farms and smallholdings owned by whites. However, it is evident that in the post-independence period, most Africans still felt that the land issue and other colonial injustices had not been resolved, even though most had established themselves well in the new settlements, such as those in the Gwai-Shangani and Gokwe areas (Alexander, MacGregor and Ranger 2000) by the time independence was achieved. The Zanu-PF government thus exploited these historical memories in their justification of their anti-Euro-American imperialism ideology and their violent seizures of land owned by white Zimbabweans. The success of the subsequent fast track land reform programme, however, is subject to controversy. The general view, based on the existence of food shortages and low production levels on the redistributed farms, is that the programme has largely been a failure, yet studies, such as Hanlon, Manjengwa and Smart's (2013) argue that it has been a success, maintaining that the 'the reality on the ground in 2012' (13) is that over 245 000 new farmers were achieving higher productivity levels. In contrast to this view, various economic historians and critics, such as Pilossof (2014) and Nyamunda (2014) heavily dispute the veracity of such pro-fast track land reform evaluations.

A Survey of Studies on Zimbabwean Fictional and Cultural Imaginaries on Land

This outline of the perceptions of and experiences on the land is also a major theme in various literary and cultural texts that have been produced in Zimbabwe throughout its literary history spanning from the 1900s to 2010. The land, in its physical sense, as both the land and the country, Zimbabwe, is dialectically linked to the social, political and personal imagination that is evident in these novels. Most of the novels, especially those describing the post-2000 invasions, represent that intricate linkage that exists between the space of the land and power; the role of the landscape in creating histories and inscribing identities, and the constitution of imaginaries and memories about land and place among white farmers and other white characters with ties to the land in Zimbabwe. Thus, as both the white and black protagonists think about their positions on place, the land and belonging, we consider Moyo's (2005:275–277) view that the land issue in Zimbabwe is both an agrarian and a social issue. In addition to Moyo's (2005) postulations, it is clear that anxieties over rights to and belonging on land and place and ultimately national belonging, aptly described as the 'reconstructions of nation and citizenship' by Hammar and Raftopoulos (2003:3), are pertinent in the analysis of the multiple perceptions and histories about land in Zimbabwe dating back to 1900.

It should be noted however that Zimbabwean fiction has long been read and studied using a methodology that is based on a segmented approach. Here, texts are categorised along race and historical periods and as a result, there is white settler fiction and African fiction; Rhodesian literature and Zimbabwean literature (Primorac 2006:13–32). Various studies that examine Zimbabwean literary history and the texts in a fragmented way where experiences on the land are examined on the basis of racial categories have indeed been published (see Chennells 1982, 1991, 1995). Themes tackled in Chennells' studies include the establishment of a racist discourse aimed at entrenching white domination over blacks and the spread of myths and propaganda about white invincibility, typified by the 'Rhodesia-never-dies' trope that dominated the white ideological perceptions during the 1960s and 1970s examined by Hancock and Godwin (1993). Also tackled in Chennells' studies, is the representation of white anxieties and their determination to establish themselves as distinct subjects striving to survive independently amidst the imperial threat from Britain and the lurking threats from the colonised blacks.

Other studies examine texts from the 1960s onwards that were written by blacks in the vernacular and English languages. The studies still take this fragmented and racially based approach to Zimbabwean writings as noted by Primorac (2006:13–32) owing to the compartmentalised pedagogical approach that has been in existence in Zimbabwean university's departments of literature and language. The best example of such a study, though not focusing on land, is Veit-Wild's (1993), which outlines the social and literary history of various black Zimbabwean writers and their works. Most important to this study of the writings on the land is Zimunya's (1982) seminal study of the African writer's imagination of land, colonialism and nationalism in colonial Zimbabwe.

Primorac (2006) takes a comparative approach in re-reading white and black Zimbabwean fiction in a comprehensive way. Primorac focuses on the inter-textual linkages and textual ideologies and novelistic time and spaces that include the Rhodesian settler and colonial experiences before and during the war of liberation. This inclusive and innovative study of Zimbabwean fiction is also evident in the collection of essays edited by Muponde and Primorac (2005), which evaluates texts written by both white and black Zimbabweans and examines emerging trends in the depiction of anti-Euro-American imperialism discourse and land in contemporary Zimbabwean literature and culture. I consider the significance of such a comparative approach in the study of Zimbabwean literature as enriching, but am nevertheless compelled to examine only the white Zimbabwean narratives about the land invasions in this book, mostly in an attempt to address the gap that exists in the critical study of post-2000 white Zimbabwean writings. I also make an attempt, albeit in a limited way, to locate black Zimbabwean writings about the land invasions in the background and juxtapose them with some of the white narratives that I examine, in an effort to show my awareness of the existence of the black voice on representations about land.

It is clear from this brief examination of the literary history and survey of some of the research on Zimbabwean fiction and culture that the history of the country and perceptions about the land are indeed central to the constitution of experiences and thoughts on belonging and social and national connectedness in Zimbabwe. I am aware in this book that ideas about identities are, as noted by Brubaker and Cooper (2000), usually used loosely and in an ambiguous way, and as such use unambiguous terms and concepts, such as categories, connectedness, shared experiences, senses of understanding and the definition of self or selves, in my examination of white Zimbabwean representations of the land invasions. For instance, it is interesting to examine how the ambiguous language and politics of identity that the Zanu-PF government used in its radical post-2000 project on land redistribution, reflected in most of the examined texts or lurking in the texts' contexts, impacted on the white commercial farmers' experiences, their sense of self, their connectedness and identification with place and nation, as well as the categorisations they earned during the campaigns. The fiction addressing such issues, especially the post-2000 white writings that are studied here, indeed attempt at addressing the issues at stake by focusing on the way white Zimbabweans constructed a sense of understanding of self and belonging in the nation. Consequently I examine how the texts studied here help us understand the nature and impact of the invasions, note how the events opened up contesting dialogues pertaining to how land is perceived, who has a right of access to it, the construction of social memories about land and who belongs on the land, as we unpack what it means to be Zimbabwean and the different categories of connectedness and sense of self that are constructed, disrupted or invoked during the post-2000 period.

Contestations over Memories about Land

The centrality of history in the contestations over the land and how issues such as race and ideology, whether white colonial or black nationalist, have been underscored as pertinent in the study of Zimbabwean literary and cultural studies. This is instructive, considering the notion of 'the muse of history' has been linked with the production of literary and cultural works as confirmed in Nyambi's (2013) study on the way the history of the Zanu-PF government has inspired a number of literary productions in Zimbabwe, especially those portraying the experiences emanating from the post-2000 crisis. Nevertheless, in the case under study here, I examine how the intersection between history and imaginings on the land have stimulated the production of white literary works that subvert the nationalist Zanu-PF elite's grand narrative and memory of land that dominates the nation and mostly black nationalists' psyche in the post-2000 period. Here, land is defined as a resource that belongs to patriotic black Zimbabweans only and has to be reclaimed, defended and imagined within the same discourse of the *Chimurenga* (war of national liberation in Zimbabwe).

The discourse of the Third *Chimurenga* is propagated through the state-sponsored media, political narratives and musical productions that were produced during this period. The musical texts by black Zimbabwean artists singing about the post-2000 land invasions and fast track land reform programme deserve a further but brief examination here, considering that this book's focus falls within the discipline of literary and cultural studies. The most outstanding musical narratives about the land are the *Hondo Yeminda* (War for the liberation of the land) *Volumes 1 and 2* (2001), by a war of national independence military veteran and musician, Comrade Chinx Chingaira and The Police Band. The double album was produced with state assistance and given priority on state radio stations during the early 2000s. It revises the old 1970s songs that were sung to boost the morale of the nationalist fighters and the colonised Zimbabweans (Pongweni 1982) by crafting new lyrics and a new political consciousness that urges black Zimbabweans to support the post-2000 land invasions. Comrade Chinx, the lead singer on the album, in a manner that underscores the Zanu-PF *Chimurenga* discourse, reminds his audience about the moment of colonial contact, the colonised blacks' loss of land and ends up singing about the last and final war seeking to liberate Zimbabwe from the remnants of Rhodesian colonialism as well as Western imperialism.

A few black fictional texts about the land invasions also exist. Some, such as Gappah's (2009) story, 'At the sound of the last post', describe the experiences of the female narrator as she remembers her past life with her politician husband who had just died and was buried at a fictional Zimbabwean National Heroes Acre shrine. The land issue is referred to at the end of this satirical story. The female protagonist agrees to the president's demand by allowing a coffin containing a bag of cement, instead of her late husband, to be buried at the national shrine, to prevent a political fallout with the Ndebele people who felt sidelined, on condition that she keeps her late husband's farm. The same focus on the post-2000 land issues is evident in Valerie Tagwira's (2007) novel through the subplot treatment of the relationship between Faith, a university student and daughter to the foreign-currency dealer Katy, and Tom, a wealthy Harare-based character. Faith's relationship with her boyfriend became strained as they argued over Tom's shady acquisition of a huge farm from a white commercial farmer, thus making an incidental reference to the post-2000 land invasions in the novel. However, Lawrence Hoba's (2009) short story collection, *The Trek and Other Stories* is one of the outstanding black Zimbabwean texts representing the post-2000 land invasions and fast track land reform. A number of stories in this collection humorously describe the struggles that some of the ordinary black Zimbabwean characters undergo on the newly acquired farms, especially their failure to engage in successful farming activities because of lack of government support and having to contend with threats and takeovers of the acquired farms by top government officials, as part of the author's satire of the Zimbabwean government's post-2000 land reform project. Furthermore, Nyaradzo Mtizira-Nondo's *The Chimurenga Protocol* (2008), which juxtaposes, in a factual historical narrative style, the colonial social and economic conditions faced by colonised Zimbabweans, especially the land expropriations and inferior education and other services, with the events occurring during the post-2000 land invasions, in an attempt to justify this controversial land reform programme, is another significant text adding to the body of black Zimbabwean narratives that fall within this book's research focus, though they are not the main subject of study, as the focus is on white writings.

However, white narratives about the land invasions examined in this study can best be examined as counter discourses to the anti-imperialist rhetoric employed by the Zanu-PF government to justify their repressive and violent land reform projects, as well as an alternative discursive space for the articulation of an alternative, literary voice (Nyambi 2013). The Zanu-PF government's anti-imperialism rhetoric, where new paradigms are used to distinguish Zimbabweans into the authentic and inauthentic, patriots and traitors, black and white, and others, are ironically drawing on the same violent and racist white discourses of the pre-1980s which ought to have been completely erased after independence was attained, as noted by Primorac (2006:76–79). Nonetheless, these contestations provide an opportunity for the crafting of subversions and new ways to understand Zimbabwe's current post-colonial condition. Evident in the post-2000 Zimbabwe condition is the agency against repression, where new discourses in the form of human rights and conservationist ideas speak against local domination and the patriotic and anti-colonial rhetoric. This is quite interesting, and as noted by Chennells (1999:126), a fitting post-colonial condition which demonstrates the simultaneous subversion of both 'the authoritarianism of the imperial centre as well as new nationalist centres'. Such a complexity should be examined as we consider the way white narratives counter the hegemonic and exclusionary Zanu-PF discourses about land.

Some of the considerations discussed in relation to the history of the country and that of the landscape, the nationalist movement and the war of liberation as well as imaginings and perceptions of the land, overlap with crucial post-colonial theoretical views. These include notions on imperialist intrusion and appropriations of the colonised land; notions of identity, anxiety, the emergence of competing discourses (colonial versus nationalist, black versus white, new black farmer versus the white commercial farmer, and the repressive government versus the human rights activists); contestations between the colonialist and the colonial subject; and the liminal positions and resistance often created as the oppressed actively engage in activities that counter the existing domination in any historical period.

While I am aware of the reversal of positions in this case, where the black Zanu-PF elite has now risen to dominance and the once-dominant white commercial farmers have been marginalised, it is still interesting to examine how the white writings speak to this experience of exclusion from the land and categorisation as Zimbabwean, and their search for alternatives and survival techniques in the face of these exclusions. The contestations over land in colonial and post-independent Zimbabwe reveal issues such as the colonial psyche of the white settlers as they perceive, name and tame the land and the colonial subjects, a process evident in Buckle (2000) and Lang's (2006) description of their efforts to establish a home and a viable farming practice in a tough environment. Other post-colonial themes include the imperial and colonial settler ideology of an open space waiting to be occupied. Here, the imperialist image, also evident in the travel writings, paintings and observations of Australia and New Zealand as discussed by Carter (1987) and McKenzie (1988), while not applying to the reality about Zimbabwe's land ownership in 2000, reminds us of the presence of the colonial discourses in the mapping of land ownership in Zimbabwe, a historical reality that the Zanu-PF elite appropriates in its campaign to justify the land invasions and its fast track land reform programme. Furthermore, these post-colonial concepts, especially the link between land and power; domination, exclusion and resistance; as well as marginalisation and the associated social-psychological and physical displacement, are considered in relation to the nature of the experiences encountered by some white landowners who are adversely affected by black nationalist discourses, and their attempts to constitute a survivalist sense of self as they to come to terms with the period's turbulence.

More so, critical moments in history, showing the first contact between Europeans and Africans as reflected in Achebe's *Things Fall Apart* (1960), Haggard's *King Solomon's Mines* (1955) and intrusion into a conquered space in the empire as reflected in Conrad's *Heart of Darkness* ([1899] 1982), are replete with the protagonists' adventures and anxieties as they try to inscribe European authority, language and perceptions from the perspective of the European beholder (Darian-Smith, Gunner and Nuttall 1996:2).

While the post-2000 Zimbabwean case is years apart from the typical Achebe and Conrad images of post-colonial contact, there is a sense in which the established conditions of post-colonial authority over natural and human resources established at the moment of contact, whose residual existences are emblematised in post-2000 Zimbabwe by white farmer's ownership of tracts of land, economic power and authority over the black farmworkers, compels us to consider the white farmer anxieties as they grapple with the loss of authority and struggle to find ways to understand the invasions and the effect that this has had on their sense of self and their sense of national belonging.

This study of white perceptions of self in times of crisis and an evaluation of whether whites can still be considered Zimbabweans in the face of exclusionary black nationalist discourses by the Zanu-PF, can still be viewed within the same lenses of post-colonial anxieties, adventures – this time adventures of loss, displacement and sometimes survival – and resistance to old intrusions on the former colonised lands, although as in the case of Buckle (2000 and 2003), the farms were not always inherited from BSAC Pioneer Column beneficiaries.

Also evident in post-colonialism are the violent colonial appropriations of the land and the entrenchment of violence in the discourse and culture of the colonised and post-independence country. This is revealed as present throughout Zimbabwe's social and historical experiences, where the land issue and the political and social fabric of the country were tainted by violence and disruptive discourses drawing on race and other divisions. One of the divisive discourses is evident in the Zanu-PF's identity politics in which they draw on what Brubaker and Cooper (2000:2–7) term loose and ambiguous categories and identifications to displace Zimbabwean white farmers and exclude black Zimbabweans, especially those who support the opposition parties, from accessing the land and other natural resources. Therefore, the book seeks to examine how white literature challenges the constructed black nationalist discourses on belonging and 'unbelonging', with the objective of testing the discourse about who is Zimbabwean and claims by white Zimbabweans to be recognised as connected to the nation and having rights to own land, the relevance of their articulation of victimhood, and to unpack the nature and impact of the invasions on being white and yet human in such a turbulent period.

Interestingly enough, the interpretation and control of historical memory has attained prominence in contemporary Zimbabwe. As the government draws on the memory of the violent colonial evictions of Africans from fertile ancestral land onto the less fertile and disease-ridden African reserves that were far away from centres of modernity, a manipulative new discourse has been created which seeks to control the imaginings of ordinary Zimbabweans and justify the violent land invasions and redistribution. This state-controlled grand narrative on the land that draws on a past historical memory punctuated by gross injustices and racially based land losses is also commonly used by claimants participating in the land restitution programme in South Africa, which has been going on for years (Walker 2008). In the case of Zimbabwe, the

Zanu-PF government propagated an ideological campaign based on the notion that the land must be returned to black Zimbabweans. Furthermore, this government perceives the white commercial farmers resisting the land redistribution and the MDC and its supporters, who do not necessarily oppose the land redistribution but the manner in which it is being carried out, as acting in complicity with white Rhodesians and the British and American imperialists.

There, however, has been a revisionist interpretation of Zimbabwe's history that has plagued Zimbabwe since 2000. This history is identified as patriotic history and its tenets include the valorisation of glories from the pre-colonial period, the virtues of the 1970s anti-colonial war and the introduction of a re-education programme, where the youth are taught about the *Chimurenga* and the heroics of Zanu-PF and the anti-imperialist ideology at high school and tertiary institutions or at the various national service camps (Ranger 2005:238–242). Patriotic history seeks to justify the land seizures and to erase the personal memories and ties to the land that are held by whites and those deemed as unpatriotic black Zimbabweans. This anti-imperialist campaign led by the Zanu-PF certainly brings forth Fanon's seminal study on 'national culture' (1963) in post-colonial studies that focuses on how the nationalist elite changes from the liberators of the nation into exploiters of the country's wealth and brutal oppressors of its citizens in the post-independence period. Nevertheless, some texts representing the issues on memory, history and the land, act as counter narratives to the state-manipulated historical memory. The texts selected and analysed represent their white writers' construction of individual and social memories over the land and the nation which counter the Zanu-PF's biased account. Interesting here is an examination of the way these white narratives are a means for whites to claim victimhood and belonging in Zimbabwe.

Imaginaries of Land in Post-2000 Zimbabwe

This study, therefore, examines white literary narratives produced between 2000 and 2010, which describe the white commercial farmers' and their relations' experiences, thoughts, memories and contestations over land in Zimbabwe. A number of questions guide this study. These are: To what extent do the narratives on land draw on and represent the power, ideological, historical and political developments taking place in Zimbabwe? In what ways do the writings portray different perceptions, aesthetics and life experiences on the land in relation to race, class and existing socio-political locations during the period under consideration? How does the representation of this turbulent Zimbabwe relate to the impact of colonialism and post-colonial nationalist governance and globalisation? To what extent do the writings reflect the various contradictions arising in the Zimbabwean social and political space? How do these contradictions relate to the development of societal and national perceptions, agencies and subversions, and projections of the country's future? What is the study's contribution to the larger solution to Zimbabwe's land question and issues about belonging? These questions guide my study of the following texts: Catherine Buckle's *African Tears: The Zimbabwean Land Invasions* (2000) and *Beyond Tears: Zimbabwe's Tragedy* (2003); Graham Lang's *Place of Birth* (2006), Christina Lamb's *House of Stone: The True Story of a Family Divided in War-Torn Zimbabwe* (2006), Buckle's *Innocent Victims: Rescuing the Stranded Animals of Zimbabwe's Farm Invasions – Meryl Harrison's Extraordinary Story* (2009), and Douglas Rogers' *The Last Resort: A Memoir of Zimbabwe* (2009).

Witnessing the Land
Invasions in *African Tears*
and *Beyond Tears*[1]

Catherine Buckle has contributed significantly towards the production of literary works that describe the experiences related to the post-2000 land invasions in Zimbabwe. The author is a Zimbabwean-born white woman, a social worker by profession and a former commercial farmer who bought some land and established herself and her family at Stow Farm, a few kilometres outside the town of Marondera and about one hundred kilometres from the Zimbabwean capital city, Harare. She rose to eminence as a writer in the Zimbabwean independent newspapers such as the *Zimbabwe Independent* and the *Financial Gazette* and internet news websites such as http://www.swradioafrica.com, through her weekly letters which catalogued the experiences that she and her family were going through when her farm fell under siege from armed Zanu-PF supporters and the veterans of Zimbabwe's nationalist war of liberation. Her two memoirs, *African Tears: The Zimbabwean Land Invasions* (2000) – here after referred to as *African Tears* – and *Beyond Tears: Zimbabwe's Tragedy* (2003) – referred to in this study as *Beyond Tears*, started off as articles that were serialised in local newspapers and other internet-based news sites. Both memoirs represent Buckle's different personalities and senses of self that she acquired during this period as she transforms from being a commercial farmer into a creative writer, an advocate of the threatened and a displaced white commercial farmer.

Buckle's work represents discourses about land and the land invasions from the realm of personal witness. The personal witness is a life writing genre, mostly in the form of a memoir, which in its description of eyewitness testimonies conflates both fact and fiction to articulate personal experiences (in most cases traumatic and hence eliciting the public's interest) during a historical moment with the objective of acquiring a better understanding of self, the events and the meaning of life during the period under focus (McNeill 2005; Jolly 2011; Stroinska and Cecchetto 2015). The memoirs are examined here to determine their significance as 'testimonial' in making us understand further the nature of events faced by Buckle and how this impacted on the constitution of identity (Stroinska and Cecchetto 2015:178–179) during the traumatic invasion of her Stow Farm and the siege of the farm house. Buckle's narratives are therefore significant in that they allow us to evaluate the different views related to the advent of the fast track land reform programme in Zimbabwe, for her memoirs are in competition with the Zanu-PF government's grand narrative about the land in post-2000 Zimbabwe.

Buckle uses the first person narrative style to represent her experiences as a white commercial farmer, wife and mother, and later as a divorcee, as well as a displaced commercial farmer and a concerned progressive Zimbabwean human rights activist and writer. She also makes some inter-textual references to television and newspaper reports in her memoirs, thus depicting how her literary productions engage in a dialogue with other genres and technologies of representation. This stylistic approach is typical of the dialogue between life writing about the personal and its linkage with the public, where the new media plays a significant role in this linkage of the personal with the public context (McCooey 2004:viiix). The non-fictive documentary style and inter-textual references employed in both memoirs therefore position her narratives as an eye-witness account seeking to break the silence about the violence, deaths, evacuations and other traumas that characterised the land invasions and the subsequent fast track land reform programme. Her narratives align themselves with characteristics of memoirs and non-fiction literary productions, which should depict the events in the named real setting accurately, with writers being expected by the readers to exercise their artistic licence to invent within limits and to strive for authenticity (Inglis 2000:69–76; Stroinska and Cecchetto 2015:178–79). Both memoirs can therefore be perceived as a literary record of a story that needed to be told truthfully as part of a counter discourse to the ruling Zanu-PF government's narrative about the land invasions and the fast track land reform programme.

The hypothetical view that guides my analysis of both memoirs is based on the incisive postulation made by Alexander (2007:183) that:

> Land is about identity as well as production and class formation; it is about aesthetic values and spiritual meaning, as well as being central to the construction of the institutions of state; it fires political struggles and violence alongside the literary imagination; and it is the basis for both building and breaking a host of social relationships. In all these guises, the meanings and value of the land are neither fixed nor uncontested. Land cannot be reduced to a static role in a single narrative.

Alexander underscores the significance of the land in the formation of identities, the creation and dislocation of social relationships and the crafting of social and imaginative aesthetics. The argument by Brubaker and Cooper (2000) calling for the use of notions and elements such as group and racial categories as well as perceptions and understandings of the self are also considered in an attempt to establish a more nuanced analysis of Alexander's views that link land to identity formation. The task then is to examine how the land invasions inspired Buckle's representations of the experiences on the commercial farms and influenced the various aesthetics and social and ideological contestations over the land in post-2000 Zimbabwe. Furthermore, the significance of Alexander's (2007) postulation that 'land ... fires political struggles and violence' should be underscored because violence figures greatly in the representations of the land invasions under focus in this study and as a result, it becomes pertinent that we examine the significance of violence in shaping the contestations over the land during both the colonial and the post-2000 eras.

Violence is at the centre of the colonial project as observed by post-colonialists. Loomba (2005:97) notes that 'military violence was used almost everywhere, although, to different degrees, to secure both occupation and trading "rights"'. Zimbabwe's colonial history from the moment of contact marked by the arrival of the Pioneer Column up to the 1970s anti-colonial war is replete with settler colonialism's use of violence to dominate over the land. This dialectical linkage between violence and colonialism in colonial Zimbabwe is depicted in various white Rhodesian novels such as WA Ballinger's *Call it Rhodesia* (1966) which describes the experiences of the chief protagonist, Alexander Strang, a member of the BSAC Pioneer Column that invaded and colonised Mashonaland and established Bulawayo; his subsequent transformation into a pioneer adventurer who traded with the Ndebele; his alliance with a weaker Shona clan, the Nakalanga, who gave him vast tracks of land as a reward for his military assistance when the Ndebele raided the Nakalanga; and how he tamed the Nakalanga and their land into one of the most successful agricultural estates in the colony from which the Strang lineage contributed, often times using violence, toward the shaping of the settler colonial dream.

Even a classical black Zimbabwean novel such as Mungoshi's *Waiting for the Rain* (1975) describes how members of the Mandengu family suffered from a displaced psyche owing to, among other factors, the legacy of their forced relocation by the Rhodesian colonial government into the drought-stricken Manyene village. In addition, a culture of violence also characterises the relationship between the white farmer and African labourers. Here, the sjambok/whip, as noted by Chennells (1991) in his examination of the fictional representations on the use of violence in colonial Rhodesia, is used as an instrument to discipline the African into civilised behaviour that respects white authority and recognises the importance of industriousness.

Ironically, the centrality of violence in maintaining power became etched in the consciousness of the colonised Zimbabweans. In addition, the colonised subjects' memory of their past heroic struggles to defend the land and their social and political independence was passed on from generation to generation. This awareness and memories became a major inspiration in the anti-colonial activism that began in the late 1950s and culminated in the anti-colonial war that raged in the 1970s.

The ambivalence of violence, a concept examined from different cultural perspectives by Aijmer and Abbink (2000), becomes evident here. That is, on one level, it is used as an instrument of conquest and control by the colonialists and on the other, it is appropriated by the colonised subjects and used to achieve liberation from the same colonial dispensation that was built through violence. Fanon (1963:31) describes this appropriation of violence by the colonised subject in an attempt to dislodge colonialism as:

> The violence which has ruled over the ordering of the colonial world, which has ceaselessly drummed the rhythm for the destruction of native social forms and broken up without reserve the system of reference of the economy, the customs of dress and external life, that same violence will be claimed and taken over by the native at the moment when, deciding to embody history in his own person, he surges into forbidden quarters.

The same appropriation of violence as a resistant practice seeking to liberate the community from colonial oppression and to reclaim the land is noted in the representations of the Mau Mau war against British colonialism in Kenya by Ngũgĩ wa Thiong'o and other writers (Maughan-Brown 1985). Therefore, memories of violent translocations and abuse perpetrated by the colonial white settlers and the creation of an ideological rhetoric that celebrated the role of violence in subverting and dislodging colonial rule dominated the psyche and national imaginary of Zimbabweans in the 1980s. It is clear here that the Zimbabwean social and political imaginary that was established after the attainment of national independence perceived 'violence as a cultural category, as a historically developed cultural form or construction' (Blok 2000:26), which they should venerate.

It is little wonder then that the Zanu-PF government began to draw on these memories to find ideological justification for the use of violence in order to defend national sovereignty against perceived threats of foreign domination. Furthermore, violence, popularly called *jambanja* by the Zimbabwean war veterans, was invoked just as 'decolonisation is always a violent phenomenon' (Fanon 1963:27), to launch what the Zanu-PF led government termed the last and final war, the Third *Chimurenga*, to reclaim the land from the white commercial farmers. Nevertheless, the ambiguities evident in the post-2000 use of the rhetoric of violence, evident in Buckle's memoirs through the inter-textual references to the press and public campaign statements by some Zanu-PF government officials and war veterans during the land invasions, should still be noted. Primorac (2006:68) notes that the violent rhetoric that was employed by the Zanu-PF officials and war veterans was racially-based and hence resonates with the Rhodesian violent oppression.

It should be underscored that issues such as the nature and the characteristics of the invasions, how they impacted on the sense of the self and social awareness, notions on national belonging in Zimbabwe and the angst of the commercial white farmers within the unfolding violent and chaotic land invasions and subsequent fast track land reform programme are analysed in relation to how they are represented in *African Tears*. The significance of both texts, especially *Beyond Tears*, in the crafting of new metaphors and perceptions on land, are also considered. The role of Buckle's work in creating new narrative styles that incorporate an activist discourse, the personal memoir style and inter-textual references to the media and internet technology in Zimbabwean literature and the country's post-colonial condition is also discussed. Hence, the major questions that are interrogated in the analysis of Buckle's two key memoirs that describe the events and impact of land invasions on white farmers and their workers, are: What are some of the characteristics of the land invasions and how did they impact on the white commercial farmers' lives, their farming spaces and perceptions of themselves and the nation? To what extent do the writings entrench and or expand on the old metaphors and other creative qualities on the writings about the land in Zimbabwean literary and cultural studies? And what is the significance of Buckle's work in the representation of the Zimbabwean post-colonial condition?

Tears and Fears during the Land Invasions

The memoir, typical of all life writing focused on personal experiences and writing about trauma (Stroinska and Cecchetto 2015:179–181), catalogues the distressing experiences that the author, her husband, Ian, and son, Richard, went through from 'Wednesday 1st March 2000' (Buckle 2000:1), the day when the news reached the protagonist and author that their property, Stow Farm, would be invaded by the veterans of the Zimbabwean war of independence. The narrator and her son were held under siege by the war veterans from March to the end of September, 2000. They were eventually forced to leave the farm for rented accommodation in the nearby town of Marondera.

In this memoir, the author lays out chapter outlines that trace the chronology of the anxiety, violence and displacement suffered by the Buckles, their farm workers and by extension their neighbours, friends and the country Zimbabwe as a whole. This is hinted at from the chapter titles: '*Hondo* (The War)'; 'The rape of the land'; 'Very, very, very severe'; 'The killing begins'; 'Trail of destruction'; 'Rivers of blood and tears'; 'Sins of the fathers'; 'Burning flesh'; 'This is my farm'; 'Fast track to where?'; 'The 3 000 'wish list''; 'Ethnic cleansing'; and '*Tawanda* and *Siya* (Leave)', which marks the end of the siege and the Buckles' decision to relocate from their farm. The narrative depicts a personal witness to the dislocating effects of the land invasions on the Buckles in a mainly literary memoir genre that also incorporates the factual documentary and inter-textual references to the media narratives and to the dialogues that the author had with institutions such as the Zimbabwe Commercial Farmers' Union (ZCFU) and the police. However, our objective in this section of the chapter is to examine the nature of the land invasions and their effect on the personal life of the author.

Buckle draws on her personal experiences and history – the Zanu-PF land invasions and land redistribution project – elements typical of memoirs and the life writing genre (Jolly 2011:366), to describe the chaos that characterised the Zanu-PF government-sanctioned post-2000 land invasions and the fast track land reform programme. This enables the readers, in a way typical of the memoir genre, to understand further what was unfolding on her farm as per the existing social and historical conditions of the period (McNeill 2005:ix).

The news of the impending invasion of Stow Farm reached Buckle through a wave of rumour. The narrator outlines how she ended up suffering from stress owing to the failure by the government to communicate directly its intentions and to produce a concrete list of farms ear-marked for expropriation and redistribution. The greater incredulity of the impending invasion is represented in the farmworkers' debate and the author's disquiet over the encroaching *Hondo* (Chapter 1 title), or war, as the invasions became associated with the discourse of the war to liberate the land (*Hondo yeminda*):

> 'But we are no designated!' Isaya said, looking to me for acknowledgement. Our farm had never been on any list for government acquisition and I hoped their doubts were right. Certainly there was nothing on our little farm that was of much interest but still we had to be prepared for an invasion and the first priority was to tighten up the security. (Buckle 2000:2)

The author constantly uses a probing narrative style, punctuated by the use of rhetorical questions and an interior monologue, in an effort to reveal the chaotic nature of the land invasions. Buckle questions why the police and the government are not doing anything to evict the 'squatters' who invaded her farm as well as those on the other farms that she has noted from the newspapers and television. The author is forced to write many letters and articles to the press and the leadership of the ZCFU, in which she criticises these institutions for their inaction and for leading the country's agricultural sector and its whole social and political sectors into disorder. Her observations of the new land-use and settlement patterns that are being established on her farm, reflected in the chapter titled 'The rape of the land', clearly underscore the author's concerns about the destruction of the landscape. Buckle outlines the disorderly new land divisions and lays out, in a letter written to a local newspaper, her perceptions of the new mappings taking place on the invaded farms:

> Two small earth dams are now 'liberated land' and I can no longer water my livestock. I have had to move all my cattle and probably only have enough grazing for another three or four weeks. The liberated land now sports 50 head of communal cattle – pushed in to graze my fields every morning. The liberated land also includes two plantations, each of 10,000 gum trees we grew to provide poles and paper for Zimbabwe.
>
> Today, 24 hours after the eviction deadline, my new neighbours hacked down 30 gum trees to build their houses – gum trees that I have nurtured for six years. They stripped bark off nearby Msasa trees to strap their shelters together. I too feel completely stripped now, of all my human rights.
>
> When is enough, enough? When will the outside world stop blaming me for being a white landowner and see this for what it really is? (Buckle 2000:19–20)

This quotation vividly depicts the enormous anxieties that the author was subjected to, as noted by her use of rhetorical questions and hence indicates, especially through the letter, the dialogue between her personal experiences and the events related to the public sphere – the land invasions (McCooey 2004: viii).

The author's sense of self and experiential conditions, which I term identity constitution criteria, is evident in her description of the personal and psychological reaction to the impending invasion of her farm. Here, I draw on Stroinska and Cecchetto's (2015:186) concept of an autobiography's 'identity protecting criteria', which are those elements always evident underneath an autobiographical text, in defining Buckle's identity constitution criteria reflected in her catalogue of experiences during the land invasions. The narrator is indeed overwhelmed by panic, helplessness and uncertainty from the moment the news about the impending invasion reaches her. The hysteria mode that she enters into is characterised by 'shaking and sobbing' (Buckle 2000:2), ordering her son, Richard, not to go to school, closing themselves in their home, changing the locks and waiting. She declares that '[t]he anticipation, and not knowing what to expect, was more stressful than anything I'd ever encountered before' (Buckle 2000:3).

The narrator suffers from further anxiety and stress after being held under siege in her farm house by a mob of whistling and singing war veterans. She at some stage describes the anxiety and distress as 'nausea of panic flooding my system' (Buckle 2000:18). She also describes how the war veterans raised the Zimbabwean flag in her field and introduced new settlers, 'almost 200 people' (Buckle 2000:18) from the nearby communal areas, Marondera and even from the capital city, Harare, who had come to occupy the recently parcelled-out plots on the farm. Both the author and the farmworkers also had to contend with the gun-wielding war veterans' extortion and demands that they leave the farm. Buckle therefore shows the way in which these anxieties disrupted their individual psyches and the family's domestic peace. The immense psychological displacement suffered by the author and the subsequent fragmented sense that she suffers, which is typical of the post-colonial experiences and senses of the self that exist in dominated spaces, are aptly captured in her journal entry as noted by the presence of terms and phrases such a 'our increased powerlessness increases every day' and 'the pain of seeing these people destroying it (the farm)' express the sense of victimhood and an ironic white othering of the invaders typical of those dislikeable colonial discourses:

> It hasn't gone away as everyone said it would; it hasn't got easier to live with or understand. The mental and psychological stress is phenomenal. The anguish and anger at our increased powerlessness increases every day. I've worked so hard these last ten years and know every inch of this farm, and the pain of seeing these people destroying it is intolerable. I feel as I imagine it must feel to be raped. Always, day after day, having to see that blue tent and the flag makes me feel violated. How can this ever end amicably? (Buckle 2000:28)

It should be emphasised that, although the criticism of the land invasions are valid and illuminating in documenting the unfolding invasion and occupations, certain contradictions, are evident in Buckle's thoughts. The chapter 'The rape of the land' elicits certain uneasiness. This is because opposing perceptions; the ones focusing on commercial and scientific agricultural practices versus those centred on the nationalist discourses that defined the land as historically and spiritually belonging to black Zimbabweans, become significant in the definition of the impact of the invasions. Buckle's displeasure at this impact emanates from perceptions resonating with cultural and scientific discourses, such as having the right amount of stock on a given grazing land (Buckle 2000:19–20), which valorise scientifically based land use plans and divisions. It thus seems as if Buckle's criticism of the invaders is located in settler colonial perceptions that define Africans as lacking scientific knowledge of agricultural practices and as indifferent to the landscape. Ranger (1999b), as noted in Chapter 2 discusses such colonial discourses in his outline of the history of the conflict between European and African perceptions of landscape and conservation in the sacred Matopos Hills in Zimbabwe. Nevertheless, the new settlers on the Buckle farm are illegal, as the farm had not been designated for compulsory acquisition by the state as required by law. Furthermore, the occupiers' land practices that include the grazing of cattle on the farm's veld and the cutting down of some of the eucalyptus and indigenous trees (Buckle 2000:19–20), are indicative of a utility-based perception of the land that is typical of subsistence agriculture. Hence, to view their activities as environmentally destructive is to miss the point and a perpetuation of those culturally based paradigms of power that post-colonial theory seeks to subvert.

Perhaps the criticism here should be directed at the government for failing to make a sound and coordinated programme that had clear support structures that would assist the new farmers to settle and map their new lands. As is rightly pointed out in the memoir, the peasants who rightfully deserved the land were forced off the land by the 'big chefs' from the Zanu-PF, the civil service, and those related to the politicians. Hoba (2009) uses a bleak tone to satirise the greedy top government officials, referred to by Buckle, in his description of the way the Mogudu family, recent beneficiaries of the fast track land reform programme in the fictional Zimbabwe's lowveld sugar plantation region of Chiredzi, is forcibly removed from the farm to give way for a police sergeant, in the story 'The second trek – going home'. Peasants, thus, became mere victims of the ruling elite and Zanu-PF's political ploy to amass wealth and remain in power.

Furthermore, the memoir makes us as 'onlookers… understand … what has happened' (Stroinska and Cecchetto 2015:177–178) during this period. As readers we become critically aware of the activities of some of the new settlers, such as the man who 'in three days … felled nearly 200 prime gums trees' (Buckle 2000:179) and the group of young men who 'were out on a hunt to roust out the last duiker, hares or guinea fowl that had escaped previous raids' (Buckle 2000:179), which can be viewed as dialectically linked with the way the Zanu-PF leadership was willing to ignore issues of national strategic concern, such as environmental sustainability, owing to their obsession with remaining in power at whatever cost. Hence, the destructive impact of the farm invaders and illegal communal hunters are not necessarily indicators of an inherent disrespect of the landscape and natural resources by African peasants and the new setters; they are instead emblems of the ensuing chaos set in motion by the power-hungry and repressive Zanu-PF machinery.

Nevertheless, Buckle's representation of the invasions shows that the government-sanctioned fast track land reform led to major environmental devastation. One must never discount the gravity of the ensuing environmental degradation that was witnessed on commercial farms such as Stow Farm, a theme also treated in Buckle's (2009) writing of Meryl Harrison's diary on her experiences as an animal rights activist during the height of the land invasions and occupations, discussed in Chapter 7. Despite the likely post-colonial uneasiness emanating from the residual white pioneer and colonial settlers' racial stereotypes that castigated the colonised Africans as indifferent to the landscape and the environment (Ranger 1999b), it should be underscored, in concurrence with the author, that a major desolation of the environment occurred in post-2000 Zimbabwe owing to the land invasions. Buckle's description of the destruction of the eucalyptus plantation, the overgrazing of her land and the random and illegal hunting of the game on her farm typify the pattern of environmental devastation occurring in the whole country during this period. She employs inter-textual references from the television and print media, thus conflating the experiential with media narratives, to describe other environmental devastations that were taking place in the country. This is noted through her observation that 'the ravages of seven months of anarchy (February to September 2000) ... would take decades to repair' (Buckle 2000:208), which she juxtaposes with excerpts from the state-owned daily newspaper, the *Herald* where the then new minister of mines, environment and tourism expressed his shock and questions the rationale behind the war veterans' slaughter of 'over 1 600 animals worth about $23 million [a huge amount, considering that the Zimbabwean dollar was still a relatively competitive currency on world currency markets at the time] in the Save Valley Conservancy during the past six months, prompting the national parks department, police and conservancy game guards to step up patrols in the area' (Buckle 2000:209). As a result, Buckle depicts the government's failure to manage the invasions and prevent the resultant environmental destruction.

However, Buckle goes on to document the absurdity of such a governmental realisation, for she juxtaposes the minister's call for increased patrols by the police and conservancy game guards in an attempt to curb the environmental devastation with another inter-textual reference to an article from the independent daily newspaper, the *Daily News*. Here, the war veteran leader from the Chiredzi region which includes the Gonarezhou National Park that is part of the transnational parks project involving South Africa and Mozambique, states that his group has cleared parts of the land in the conservancy and declared it out of reach to any ranch scouts (Buckle 2000:209). The author, thus, depicts the ineffectiveness of the government in controlling these invasions.

In fact, Buckle captures the chaotic nature of the invasions and the fast track land reform programme. This is reflected in the revelation that various commercial farmers had initiated collaborative conservancy programmes with the local communities and their district councils, and as a result, the ensuing invasions disrupted all the functional conservation structures in place. Furthermore, even the government, as noted by the author, placed game and safari ranches on its gazetted list of farms for compulsory acquisition in the Marondera region and the rest of the country. This, therefore, confirms, as metaphorically noted by Buckle, that the land invasions went hand in hand with the rape of the land, natural forests and wild game on the white-owned commercial farms. This adds to the creation of an image of the farming and conservancy landscape tottering towards an environmental, social and economic apocalypse. It should be noted that the environmental degradation and the accompanying disregard of the farmlands' animal populations, witnessed during the invasions, is captured in both *African Tears* and *Beyond Tears*, and other texts. This is evidenced by the representations of the mercy killings of abandoned pets, horses, and other farm animals that had to be carried out while the farms were under siege or had been hurriedly deserted by their original owners, as diarised by Meryl Harrison (2009).

Buckle's memoir is indeed critical of the government-sanctioned land invasions. She uses a probing style that is indicated by the use of rhetorical questions and an investigative tone to register her criticism of the land invasions, in a way that resonates with Jolly's (2011) notion of the dissent common in activist life stories. The author searches for information and analyses it to assess the government's decisions, the politicians' and farmer organisations' press statements and the implications behind the government gazettes designating the listed farms. In this way the memoir engages in a dialogue with various narrative points and perceptions about land and the fast track land reform programme. Furthermore, her agency is noted through letters written to the local independent newspapers and foreign media to make society aware of some of the horrible experiences that were occurring on the farms under invasion. A particular beauty implied in this book, is the fact that the invasions and her position of being a white commercial farmer enables her to tap away at her keyboard from her besieged position and acquire the strength to create discourses that counter the Zanu-PF's grand narrative about the fast track land reform programme. This is noted, for instance, in her cataloguing of her letters to the editor and the very production of 'this book to tell the story of one family's struggle against state-sponsored terror' (Buckle 2000:xi) to the world. This narrative agency is therefore analogous to the post-colonial notion of writing against domination wherever it exists (Chennells 1999; Ashcroft, Griffiths and Tiffin 1995).

The author also uses awkward and sometimes contrasting juxtapositions that pre-empt, and in the process subvert, the Zanu-PF grand narrative on the land reform. The first of such juxtapositions is noted in the way her family's experiences at the hands of the violent land invaders, are linked to the violence and chaos at other farms. For example, the first chapter which dramatically introduces the reader to the encroaching land invasion and the hysteria that the writer goes through as she secures herself and waits for the eventual invasion, is followed by a chapter that refers to the actual newspaper articles describing the invasions that were occurring in other parts of this Zimbabwe. Events are also linked in a manner that undermines the state's grand narrative. Chapter 3, 'Very, very, very severe', for instance describes the interest that was engendered among the foreign press owing to the journal that Buckle was emailing to the world beyond her besieged farm house. However, as the chapter unfolds, a description of the anxiety that Buckle undergoes after realising that her son, Richard, had been stressed and traumatised by the activities of the war veterans and supporters of the ruling government who had occupied Stow Farm, is juxtaposed with an inter-textual reference to President Mugabe's warning that there would be '" very, very, very severe" consequences against white farmers if they tried to fight back' (Buckle 2000:29). This clearly shows the way in which people like the Buckles were rendered vulnerable. In addition, the juxtapositions emblematise the contradictions that were inherent in the fast track land reform programme and thus serve as a stylistic and structural indicator of the condemnation of the state narrative that justified the fast track land reform as just and considered it as an organised process.

Buckle also subverts the Zanu-PF black nationalist grand narrative that the land invasions are the third and final war aimed at speeding up the process of returning land stolen by whites during the colonial period to the black Zimbabweans so that the nation can attain social and economic prosperity. The dominance of this grand narrative in the post-2000 land invasions and national politics is depicted in the memoir through references to some press statements made by government ministers, notably the then minister of information, Professor Jonathan Moyo, the late leader of the Zimbabwe War Veterans Association, Chenjerai Hitler Hunzvi, and President Mugabe's Independence Day celebration addresses and other press conferences. These are juxtaposed with the events on Stow Farm and others in the country that are characterised by violence, chaos and the betrayal of the peasants who needed the land the most. Buckle also describes how the grand narrative about the fast track land reform became synonymous with the Zanu-PF government's extortion of some of the commercial farmers and the holding of violent political campaigns seeking to indoctrinate and intimidate farmworkers and peasants so that they would vote for their party in the parliamentary elections of 2000. This is clearly revealed in the following exclamations made by one of the war veterans who was forcing Buckle (2000:136–137) to release her farmworkers so that they could attend a Zanu-PF campaign rally:

'This is my farm,' the ringleader said speaking very slowly and loudly. 'This is my farm and this is my fields.' […]

'This is my farm.'

'Oh.'

'This is my cows.' [...]

'This is my farm, this is my fields, this is my grass, this my cow.'[...]

'Yes, I understand,' I said, my voice choked, quavering. 'But what is it that you want?'

'Give me your workers, NOW!' he screamed at me through the oh so fragile gate. 'NOW, give them now.' He wanted our workers to attend the meeting that was getting underway down in the field. [...]

'That store there,' he bellowed, pointing vaguely in the right direction, 'that store it is for Africans. We are Africans, you whites, all you whites you fuck off to Britain.'

The above conversation typifies the emotionally charged and sometimes incoherent discourse, invoking some macabre humour, which was employed by the war veterans and the Zanu-PF government to undermine the commercial farmers' role, presence and access to the land.

This incoherence is by extension a metaphor of the irrationality that characterises the land invasions that are so vividly described by Buckle from an experiential point of view. The author demonstrates that though the land reform is historically justified in order to address the residual legacy of colonialism, the events and outcomes taking place on the occupied farms were at times irrational to the extent that they should be condemned and be exposed to the world. She notes that from February to the end of September 2000, 'many people had now claimed they were in charge of this [her] farm' (Buckle 2000:180). She also documents the shock and disbelief that was felt by foreign and local journalists after their discovery of the truth about her citizenship and ownership rights to the farm:

> The journalists came (from Sudan, Nigeria, South Africa, Britain and Zimbabwe) to record the remaining fragments of our farm. [...] They didn't ask many questions but the ones that did, were repetitions of my words and already told story. You mean you were born in Zimbabwe? You were educated in Zimbabwe? You did not inherit this farm? You bought the farm ten years after independence? You got a Certificate of No Interest from the Zimbabwe Government? This farm is not designated? You have not been listed for acquisition? Your property has not been gazetted for confiscation? The police will not remove the war veterans? [...] As each group of reporters left, they wished us well, offered their condolences, empathised with our pain. There were black and white reporters and, as we did, just shook their heads sadly. (Buckle 2000:223–224)

In this way the author clearly depicts the chaotic nature of the land invasions and its grounding on a feeble and self-serving campaign that sought to undermine other narratives and manipulate the nation's memories. This exposé of the 'truth' thus becomes Buckle's vehicle to subvert the state's land reform project as defined by the Zanu-PF government.

Buckle also portrays the violence that characterised the land invasions. The war veterans, the main characters in the land invasions, retrieved the militant and anti-colonial discourse from the 1970s anti-colonial war and thus defined the invasions as the final war to liberate the land from white Rhodesian and Euro-American control. They also reproduced discourses of mass militancy and mobilisation from the past as they consolidated their occupation of Stow and other farms. As a result, farmworkers were subjected to all-night political re-education programmes. Those deemed sell-outs, such as Jane, a worker at Buckle's farm store, were severely beaten.

It is little wonder that Buckle is reduced to a nervous wreck when the war chant, signalling the beginning of her farm's invasion, is made. The Buckles are violated psychologically through the constant and intimidating surveillance by the omnipresent war veterans who occupied their farm. Violent threats became the order of the day. Even other farmers from the nearby farms in the Marondera and Macheke farming areas, as well as in other parts of the country, were beaten with iron rods, fists and even shot at, as outlined in the memoir. As a result, Buckle manages to subvert the state's narrative about the moral and political justification of the land invasions and fast track land reform by laying bare her observations, in memoir form, which readers have to take as the actual facts about the events on the farms, as noted in the chapters titled 'The killing begins' and 'Sins of the fathers'. In addition, the dedication page of the memoir honours those people who were killed by the war veterans, the youth militia and some Zanu-PF supporters since 2000, just as Pilossof (2012) does in his historical text where he lists a number of white farmers killed during the land invasions and the fast track land reform programme. Hence, the land invasions and the subsequent fast track land reform programme are represented as a nationalist project, severely punctuated by politically motivated violence, which in effect subverts the Zanu-PF justification of the land invasions as a patriotic project; for Buckle shows that coercion and the pursuit of self-interests shaped the way the land issue was addressed on the farms.

The violence that Buckle documents, can be viewed as emblematic of a conflict about perceptions on national belonging or national identity, as postulated by Alexander (2007:183). Different notions of what constitutes national identity, among them whether a community shares the same consumption patterns, imagine themselves as united by a similar experience, share the same geographical and historical background, use the same language or are of the same race, which are akin to Anderson's (1986) views on identity formation, are rekindled on the farms in post-2000 Zimbabwe. In the memoirs, inter-textual references to media representations refer to the Zanu-PF race-based categorisations which proclaimed that black Zimbabweans have a historical right to the land. This discourse on historical rights is used by the state and the invaders to redefine notions of national identity at political rallies, on the farms and in the various media platforms. As a result, blackness signifies one's organic links with Africa, an 'authentic' Zimbabwean identity and an entitlement to the land, while whiteness becomes synonymous with Europe, foreignness and an absence of rights to own land in Zimbabwe (Raftopoulos 2003, 2004; Muponde 2004). This link between the contestations over identity and belonging, with notions on race-based categories and the anti-Western imperialism agenda that figured in the discourses about the land invasions is described thus by Buckle:

> Pressure was beginning to mount though as the European leaders urged an end to the farm invasions and a restoration of law and order. By now it had become blatantly clear though, that it was a highly charged political manoeuvre and was not going to be easy to stop. It became even more frightening when a senior official from the War Veterans' Association played the next card of what was appearing to be a master plan. The first card had been land, the second was race. Whites, farmers in particular, were accused of attempting to return the country to its previous status of being a colony. (Buckle 2000:17)

Therefore, a white commercial farmer such as Cathy Buckle, who struggles to assert her views and sense of belonging through her letters to some news article editors and farmer organisation leaders, is thus identified, in the discourse on land invasions, as a target for exclusion from the land.

This definition of the land invasions and the fast track land reform programme with racial and citizenship categories, where white commercial farmers were perceived as the foreign other in Zimbabwe, point to an interesting contradiction. The discourse of alterity that is employed by the Zanu-PF government to exclude white commercial farmers from accessing and belonging on the land is located in the old colonial discourses that are similar to those used by the colonial Rhodesian government. Primorac (2006) examines this post-colonial contradiction where the ruling elite draw on colonial discourse as the Rhodesian chronotope. The ultimate intention was to transport the commercial farmers into the realm of the excluded and foreign who did not deserve to own the land in Zimbabwe because the land 'belonged' to black Zimbabweans and this undermined the plausible discourse of national reconciliation that defined the immediate post-1980 Zimbabwe.

Buckle also documents the dislocating effects of the land invasions. The author captures the psychological displacement and the subsequent fragmentation that the narrator suffered. She enters into a panic-driven life rhythm after receiving rumours about the impending invasion of her farm as she describes: 'So now with all these things to carry, four dogs to coax into the house and the gates to lock, I reached the edge of hysteria' (Buckle 2000:5). Furthermore, as noted in both memoirs, the war veterans could arrive suddenly, burn the farmland and in the process force the farmers to engage in mass evacuations. They could also surround the farmhouses and attack the farmers using guns as they did to Martin Olds on his farm outside Bulawayo (Buckle 2000:54–55). This forced farmers to enter into a new and disturbed social and spatial zone, where they were vulnerable subjects. Worse still, movements were now determined by the war veterans, who could invade the farms and displace the farmers. In her email to her 'family and friends', Buckle ponders on the kidnapping of the Macheke-based farmer, David Stevens, his forced displacement to the Murehwa district war veterans' office and police station, and his subsequent death as a result of the brutal assaults suffered during this horrific incident (Buckle 2000:62–63). This event is vividly described in the chapter aptly titled 'Murehwa – The weekend from hell' in *Beyond Tears*. This represents the disturbed space that the commercial farmers were forced to occupy owing to the farm invasions. Even the farms themselves were turned into circumscribed territories, noted by Buckle as 'No-go areas for whites' (Buckle 2003:111), as the war veterans barricaded farms from the rightful owners. Sometimes they would disrupt all farming activities and yet the police would not intervene to protect the poor, vulnerable farmers. This creation of new boundaries on the commercial farms and the imposition of new directions and centres of focus in the farmers' lives are depicted in Buckle's memoirs as indicative of the displacement and vulnerabilities that some of the white commercial farmers acquired during the post-2000 land invasions.

The stress arising from the pressure associated with the invasion and siege of the farmhouse leads to the creation of inner and psychological displacement within Cathy, her husband and son, Richard. Buckle captures the psychological turmoil she suffered by recounting her 'terrified and traumatised' call to her mother where she implores her not to visit the threatened farm. 'The anguish and anger at our increased powerlessness increase everyday' (Buckle 2000:28). Buckle also realises how their lives have been turned upside down owing to the land invasions:

> 'Oh,' he [Richard] said, thought for a moment and then continued, 'Is it in case the war vets come and try and take our house?'
>
> I didn't know what to say so I just hugged him and told him to go and play with Linnet. So wrapped up in our own panic and the collapse of law and order, the loss of our business, our livelihood and perhaps even our home, I had paid precious little attention to the fears of our son. I had no idea he knew as much as he obviously did, didn't realize that all horrors we saw on television, of war veterans evicting people from their homes,

he saw too – and understood what he was seeing. What a mess I thought.
Our lives were falling apart, piece-by-piece. (Buckle 2000:26–27)

The toll of the psychological displacement brought about by the farm invasions put the Buckles' marriage under pressure and later culminated in divorce as she points out in *Beyond Tears*. This confirms how the effects of the invasions also encroached into the space of the domestic relations of some of the victimised commercial farmers. In fact, both texts portray how the deaths of some of the white commercial farmers, such as Steven, left young families without fathers, thus underscoring the multiple displacements arising out of the land invasions that Buckle represents in her narratives.

The Buckles were also displaced physically. They finally relocate to rented accommodation in the nearby town of Marondera. The forced relocation to Marondera is expressed in an apocalyptic tone: 'And so, for me, it was over' (Buckle 2000:229). The experiences are depicted as a family tragedy and one easily empathises with her loss, considering that she and her family's terrible experiences are a personal account of an ordinary and hard-working commercial farmer whose only crime was that she is white and easily dispensable in the arena of black nationalist post-colonial politics.

Another angle to the story is that Buckle has a warm and caring relationship with her farm workers and their children. She gave her farmworkers some of the money realised from the sale of her movable property as a severance package and also gave some of the workers' children toys and other parting gifts. She also handled the closing up operations and processes with her workers in a very humane way as noted here:

If the partings so far had been painful, it was nothing compared to the anguish of saying goodbye to the people who had so faithfully worked with and for me over the last decade. Each person received a large envelope and in it was everything that I was required by law to give them, as well as whatever I could spare. The proceeds from the sale of all bits and pieces sold in the store had been shared out, as had the money from the sheep that had been slaughtered. It was a sizeable amount on its own, not much though, when split eight ways. [...] I spoke to each person in turn, thanking them for everything, wishing them luck and health and happiness in whatever the future held for them, wherever they might be. I would not forget them – not for a very long time. We had shared so much, joy and pain. I was no longer ashamed to let them see my tears. (Buckle 2000:229)

This invocation of the end of an era – 'it was over' – (Buckle 2000:229) and the humane way she parts with her workers, also confirmed by her neighbours and the public taxi drivers who plied the route linking her farm and Marondera, can be viewed as a counter-perception that subverts the overarching black nationalist discourse that categorised white commercial farmers as a group of cold and exploitative racist masters. It also highlights the plight of the farmworkers who lost their jobs and became homeless as a result of the land invasions.

The tragedy faced by the Buckles at their farm is linked to an apocalyptic image of a post-2000 Zimbabwean condition. The memoir reflects indicators of an unfolding economic collapse through references to the low tobacco sales that were made in 2000; the subsequent propagandist accusations by Minister Mujuru that farmers were destroying their crop rather than selling it on the auction floors in an attempt to sabotage the economy; and the invasion and closure of business at important agro-based companies such as the timber-producing Border Timbers (Buckle 2000:96–97). Buckle also describes in *Beyond Tears* how a number of Zimbabweans, especially the urban dwellers, including children and the sick, were beginning to be affected by food shortages, a strand also treated by black Zimbabwean writers such as Tagwira (2007) and Gappah (2009). She depicts further that major state hospitals, such as Harare Central Hospital, were severely affected by shortages of drugs and food for the patients.

This infrastructural collapse was even worsened by the disruptive activities of the war veterans where government officials who were known to be, or suspected to be, sympathisers of the opposition MDC were dismissed summarily as evidenced by the events that occurred at the national referral hospital, Parirenyatwa, (Buckle 2003:81). Buckle depicts the collapse as extending into the country's service sectors where 'water pumps in Ruwa broke down and thousands of homes had no water. [...] Telephone lines to dozens of farms in and around Marondera were out of order' (Buckle 2003:157). The texts that were produced later, such as Tagwira's *Uncertainty of Hope* (2007) and Godwin's memoir, *When a Crocodile Eats the Sun* (2006) describe the social and economic difficulties that were faced by some residents of Harare and of other parts of the country owing to the huge economic downturn as the crisis raged. This points to the fact that the violent disruptions which had displaced farmers such as Buckle, did not only mean an end to the livelihoods of these white farmers, but also marked the beginning of the dislocation of the country's social and economic sectors from as early as mid-2000.

The displacement is also revealed as wide-ranging. A number of white farmers were forced to abandon their farms and to move to cities in Zimbabwe and even to foreign countries, including South Africa. The farm invasions thus brought in a twist of forced local and international migration out of Zimbabwe. This complicated post-colonial condition has subsequently led to the creation of restless, dislocated and fugitive identities in a number of displaced white commercial farmers, their workers and some ordinary black Zimbabweans. Buckle's writings, especially, *Beyond Tears*, are a meta-narrative of the fragmentation and grappling with a fugitive status at some stage, as noted in the first chapter of *Beyond Tears*, where she describes her fears that she was under surveillance from the notorious state intelligence agency and would likely be brutalised or imprisoned for having spoken and written against the land invasions. Hence, the forced migrations and the associated labelling, as the foreign other, forced Buckle and other white farmers to review their perceptions of national belonging and citizenship. Worse still the whole country became socially, politically and economically fragmented. This complex individual and societal dislocation is portrayed in Buckle's statement here:

> By the end of May 2002 I did not know if I still belonged or was wanted in the country of my birth. I knew that the madness could not go on much longer and that the economy had almost completely collapsed. As each farmer was chased out and as every business closed down the loss to the country was enormous – in skills, expertise, taxes and revenue. Zimbabwe stood as a fragmented nation with divisions at every level. (Buckle 2003:157)

Conclusion

Buckle's writings, therefore, document the tragic experiences that ordinary white farmers, such as the author herself, went through during the height of the post-2000 farm invasions. The chaos and contradictions evident in the represented land invasions not only depict the fragmentation of some members of the white commercial farmers, but also points to a possible apocalyptic social, economic and political trajectory of post-2000

Zimbabwe. It is little wonder then that the titles of both memoirs invoke a bleak sense of loss, as signified in the tears of *African Tears* (2000) and affirmation of the tragic nature of the events as noted in the subtitle of 'Zimbabwe's tragedy' in *Beyond Tears* (2003).

Nevertheless, Buckle reveals her resilience as a writer, in that her works document what she terms the 'true' events happening on the farms and parts of Zimbabwe as is typical of non-fiction, much to the displeasure of the dominant and repressive government's attempts to suppress the spread of narratives about these violent and absurd experiences taking place on the invaded farms. She depicts further the possibility, now affordable in the Zimbabwean literary production, to extend one's creative aesthetics through the incorporation of multiple perspectives, different styles and use of inter-textual references. These multiplicities, typical of post-modernist and post-colonial writings, are indicated in the presence of the factual, personal memoir, contemporary historical tone and the interlinks between the author's experiences and the new media and print technology that assist the author to aptly capture the twenty-first century Zimbabwean experiences about land. The fluid and complex style, which is mostly a bricolage of fact and fiction, different histories and memories is indeed an appropriate and bold attempt at representing the experiences that some of the white commercial farmers, their workers and ordinary Zimbabweans encountered. The social and historical imaginary thus intersect but the author ably represents to us, in a way that wins our trust, the events related with the social and political re-mappings initiated through the post-2000 land invasions and in the process provokes us to think about the possibilities of crafting a complex and inclusive national narrative on connectedness to land and nation and belonging that respects difference.

Notes

1. An earlier version of this chapter was published in *Journal of Literary Studies*, 27(2) 2011.

Memory-making and the Land in Graham Lang's *Place of Birth*

Graham Lang's *Place of Birth*, written from the perspective of Vaughn Bourke, a white Rhodesian expatriate and naturalised citizen of Australia, departs from the memoir style representations of the post-2000 land invasions discussed in Chapter 3. Lang's novel carries a literary view and tone that is perhaps liberal in nature. Vaughn Bourke, the narrator, admits in the early stages of the narrative that he stood aloof during the early stages of the land invasions as he was of the opinion that the subsequent fast-track 'redistribution of white-owned farming land to black farmers was not only inevitable, but historically just' (Lang 2006:17). He, however, had to get rid of this sense of detachment when the invasions became violent and murderous. Nevertheless, Vaughn's narrative is characterised by a tone that hovers between aloofness and an outsider's openness.

The novel describes Vaughn's views, within the thematic paradigm on place and dislocation (Macgregor 2006), as he encounters different experiences during the period when the family farm lay under siege from invading war veterans in 2005. During this period, he reunites with his brother Angus, a former member of the notorious Rhodesian military branch called the Selous Scouts who is presently displaced from the family farm called Hopelands. Vaughn also reunites with his sister Angela, a wildlife artist resident in the United Kingdom. The siblings also engage in hard labour to exhume their ancestors from the graves on the farm that were under threat from the war veterans, so that they can rebury them at a safe cemetery in Shangani. The siblings also get involved in other adventures as they travel to and from Hopelands. These include dealing with the omnipresent violent war veterans waiting to take over the farm as soon as the exhumations and reburials are over. The key issues Lang treats here are the effects of the land invasions on family histories, personal memories and family relations.

The novel also dwells on the predicament that white Zimbabweans with ties to the land face as black Zimbabweans, especially the nationalist Zanu-PF, ideologically redefine what it means to be and what is expected of a Zimbabwean. The redefinition is exclusionary. The notions certainly contrast with Anderson's (1986) postulation that the sharing of similar geographical, historical, language and consumption patterns plays a significant role in the constitution of imagined communities and identities. Thus the evident irony here is that although some whites, such as the Bourkes, claim citizenship by birth, their family histories about their ancestors' involvement in the colonial expropriation of the land from the indigenous communities and their later involvement in the fight to fend off the nationalist military fighters in the 1970s, leads to their exclusion from the national imaginary and categories of perceptions on citizenship that were being propagated by Zanu-PF.

The chief protagonist in the novel, Vaughn, describes his experiences in Zimbabwe after his return 'to [his] place of birth for the first time in twenty-six years' (Lang 2006:5). His perspectives, during this period, are drawn from events related to the family reunion, memories about childhood and experiences from his upbringing at Hopelands Farm in the old Rhodesia. The theme of childhood memories on the land, which are mostly represented in a nostalgic way that portrays 'an overly romanticised vision of the farm setting and of life before the land invasions started' (Pilossof 2009), is common in autobiographical texts and memoirs written by whites before the land invasions, as noted by Harris (2005). This theme is also treated in post-2000 narratives written by other white writers. Holding's novel *Unfeeling* (2005) describes how the chief character, Davey Barker, is orphaned after his parents were violently murdered by a group of farm invaders, turns to the memories of his early childhood experiences on the farm and the pastoral life before the invasion, as a way of dealing with the trauma associated with his tragic condition. The same thematic strand is evident in the way Nigel Hough, a recently dispossessed white farmer, recounts his early childhood on his parents' farm and his farming experiences on the farm before it was invaded in 2002, as documented by Lamb (2006) in *House of Stone*. Similarly, Lang describes the experiences that Vaughn went through after his return to Zimbabwe and in the process treats themes such as the land and its meaning to the Bourke family lineage, its effect on perceptions and understandings of the self and the role of the past (Rhodesia) on belonging and coming to terms with the experiences unfolding after 2000.

It should be underscored that the land issue is central to the experiences of the Bourke siblings. Place and land intersect in the novel and are portrayed as playing a major role in either displacing, holding or drawing back the siblings at various stages in their lives. Lang acknowledged that this theme is one of his major literary preoccupations in an interview with Macgregor (2006). The siblings' reunion comes after a very long period of family dislocation. Vaughn's sense of belonging in colonial Zimbabwe was disrupted by the bush war waged by the nationalist fighters in order to reclaim the land from colonial Rhodesian control, which he opposed. His liberal sentiments are noted in the flash-back scenes describing his student days at university where he engaged in anti-colonial and anti-apartheid activism. Even during his current return, he narrates his observations on the conflict over the land issue with Angus, who strongly believes in his family's right to own Hopelands Farm. Angus is ready to form alliances for convenience, as shown in the one he forms with Saxon – a former freedom fighter whom he allied with during the invasions to create the impression that the farm was now under black Zimbabwean ownership. He is also prepared to fight in order to keep the land in the family and not let it be acquired by the war veterans, as discussed later in this chapter. Alexander's (2007:183) postulations that land is central to the production of identity, class, aesthetic values, social and political meanings, and literary writings, is considered in the analysis of the experiences of the Bourkes.

Finally, the act of exhuming the remains of the Bourke ancestors from their graves, a significant event in the plot, becomes a metaphor for the excavation of personal and family memories and history in the novel. An archive of the memories and accounts of the family's experiences during the colonisation of the land and the establishment of personal links with the land are retrieved during the exhumation and other experiences on the farm and in Bulawayo during the reunion. These siblings also talk about the 1970s nationalist liberation war, the politics about the ownership of resources such as the land, and the resultant tragic death of their parents during a farm attack led by the nationalist military fighters. The surviving Bourkes' experiences are also indicative of a re-making of family alliances, as the siblings have been dislocated for years. Thus, the novel depicts the siblings' journey towards memory retrieval, the remaking of family and other alliances within a larger social, historical and psychological space where all whites with a stake in and linkages to any farmland, have to re-evaluate their views of the self and belonging in post-2000 Zimbabwe. In fact, the Bourkes' experiences here invoke Ranger's (2005:219) view that 'history matters in Zimbabwe' as the Zanu-PF determined the narrative and constructed it into a monolithic one, even though Zimbabwean history has always been shifting as noted by Nyamunda (2014). This particular Bourke family history can thus be viewed as an indictment of the simplistic black nationalist history that erases the presence of other histories during this ideologically contested period. Furthermore, the Bourkes also constantly grapple with the threat of violence and the social and physical dislocation that characterises experiences associated with the land issue as represented in the novel.

This chapter therefore seeks to examine the contestations between a dominant state and the individual or family definition of the self and connections to the nation as well as the significance of the land as represented in Lang's novel *Place of Birth*. Also considered are the intricate linkages between the land and memories and social dislocations constituted within the depicted white commercial farmers.

The Land, Dislocation and Memory

Vaughn and Angela's' return to Zimbabwe leads to a reunion with the other sibling Angus. This triggers a process of memory-making among the Bourkes. The siblings recollect what they consider, from a colonial perspective, as their ancestors' significant contribution to the taming of the colonial landscape into a viable farm. The recollections resonate with Chennells (1982:235–257) and Pilossof's (2012) discussions on the representations and history, respectively, of the early white settlers and how they survived the brooding African jungle and worked hard to establish what Chennells considers as the foundation of the image of a Rhodesian identity that has strong ties with the farmland. They also remember their childhood experiences on the farm, personal experiences away from the farm and on the farm in post-independence Zimbabwe. The novel outlines the reunion and chaotic experiences that the Bourkes encounter during the land invasions, including the tragic death of Angela. As depicted in Buckle's memoirs (2000;2003), the land invasions were linked to the politics about the land issue in post-2000 Zimbabwe and characterised by the looting of farm products, the use of abusive language, extortion, harassment and the violation of farmworkers and the farmer.

The Bourkes' current experiences, their sense of self and history, as reflected through flashback scenes and the protagonists' memory-making, are all tied to Hopelands Farm. The farm and its history are portrayed as significant in the mapping of a Rhodesian identity. It also unites the Bourkes as a family because the farm had been passed from one generation to the other, as expressed by the narrator here:

> My family, the Bourkes, were regarded as 'old Rhodesians' because we were among the first settlers in Matabeleland. We have owned and occupied a farm called Hopelands near the railway siding settlement of Shangani since 1897, just after the *Chimurenga* Rebellion. I was born a fourth-generation Rhodesian, the youngest of three children: Angela, Angus and me, Vaughn. (Lang 2006:13)

This novel is therefore, significant in that the protagonists' history and experiences are interlinked with issues such as the existence of a past history of white settler appropriation of the indigenous communities' land and the colonial historiography associated with the constitution of Rhodesian identity that most white Zimbabweans find difficult to shed. Furthermore, the reaction and perspectives of white characters such as the Bourke siblings is quite critical in this study of the literary and cultural representations of experiences about the post-2000 land invasions.

The farm is mapped as a vital space in the siblings' life in that Vaughn describes it as a home and a familiar landscape. The drive to Hopelands can be viewed as a metaphor of Vaughn's journey towards reclamation of and reconnection with home and the familiar. The arrival at Shangani, a farming settlement near their farm, ignites a nostalgic identification with the place. The narrator describes Shangani as his tiny 'hometown' and notes its significance as a secure shopping and farmer's meeting point for social gatherings, as they grew up. A similar attachment with the landscape and farm is also depicted in Holding's *Unfeeling* through the way Davey constantly seeks attachment with and remembrances of his parents' farm and its landscape during his return to seek vengeance over the killing of his parents during an invasion of their farm. The narrator of *Place of Birth*, however, describes the farm landscapes in a romanticised tone (Pilossof 2009; 2012) that depicts his intimate linkage with the farm. He describes from a high point suitable for a wide gaze how the nearby river flows towards the Zambezi, and how the skies, plains and mountains merge to form a seamless beauty of merged rock and vegetation. The stance and tone are reminiscent of the colonialist's perception of the colonised land, typical of the post-colonial imperial gaze. This line of thinking positions the commercial farmer and white Zimbabwean's ties to the land as intimate, but somehow tinged with the aura of a romanticised aesthetic linkage to the land, rather than its utilitarian value.

Pilossof (2009:630) considers the way whites connect with 'the land, and the beauty of the farm and its setting' as contradictory because most of the whites do not connect very well with the blacks on the farms, a view also pointed out by Hughes (2010) in his historical outline of how white Rhodesian farmers preferred to connect with the African landscape rather than with their black workers. This narrative focus on the master-servant relationship on the farm is treated in the novel through the siblings' relationship with the old Ndebele couple, Joseph and Anna, who were first employed by their parents. Even though there is an element of a close relationship between the masters and the servants, the latter are represented as meek and docile workers. More importantly, in a manner that agrees with Pilossof's (2009) assertion that white farmers did not have a connection with their black workers, the Bourke siblings regard the workers as incidental to their lives.

On the day of their arrival back at the farm the Bourkes are seen to be greatly attached to and fascinated with the symbolic fixtures that were established there, judging by the length of the narrative of the incident. These included the farmhouse itself that was built over a long time by the different Bourke generations and the ten-metre cross erected by the siblings' grandfather on a hill, which became known as the Long-Cross Hill, after the siblings' father had returned alive at the end of the Second World War. This shows that the Bourkes had cultivated a close linkage with the environment and landscape of Hopelands, in a typical white and Rhodesian attachment with the land as discussed by Chennells (1982).

The existence of this close sense of belonging to the farm explains the anxieties felt by some of the white characters during the land invasions. The Bourke siblings are unnerved by the new mappings on the farm, the war veterans' squatter camps, which compete with the traditional white farmer and the family's nodes such as Long-Cross Hill. Lang also describes most of the routes to and from the white farming spaces as having been transformed into disrupted ones bearing similarities with war zones. This is illustrated in the novel through the ubiquity of road blocks along the major roads where whites and blacks suspected of opposing the fast track land reforms and of being supporters of the opposition MDC were interrogated or harassed by the armed war veterans. For instance, Vaughn is interrogated for being an Australian passport-holder and extorted of his foreign currency by war veterans at a road block along the Shangani-Bulawayo road. Some of the farms around Shangani, where the Bourke's farm is located, are transformed into disrupted and abandoned spaces. There are also murders of some farmers as exemplified in the narrative through the tragic deaths at Gerber's farm, which neighbours Hopelands.

This chaos and violence engenders restlessness within the Bourke siblings that is symbolised by the numerous heated debates that Vaughn and Angus have, in which the former believes, in a typically ex-patriate perception, that Africa belongs to the Africans and all that Angus has to do is 'to pack up and walk away' (Lang 2006:179). The frequent arguments between the Bourke brothers; the tension between Angus and his wife, Jenny, over Angus' visits to Hopelands; and his refusal to migrate to the West, express the anxiety affecting some of the white characters in this novel. The irony of such an anxiety is that this is not the usual anxious condition of the colonised subject, as noted by Fanon (1963), but rather an anxiety existing in the displaced white citizens and commercial farmers owing to the invasions occurring in post-2000 Zimbabwe. Angus, who as noted by Anna, 'cannot live without the farm' (Lang 2006:177) asserts that the farm is his place too (Lang 2006:179). This is a symbolic indicator of the Bourkes' perceived right to belong on the land and in this country, like other white Zimbabweans such as Buckle (2000;2003) and Nigel Hough (Lamb 2006). It also reveals the existence of this muted defiance against the racially-based politics of identity and rights to the land. It implicitly shows the need for Zimbabwe's post-colonial political elite to accept a wide-ranging and inclusive idea of how people from different racial and ethnic categories as well as different political persuasions can connect together and with the nation.

The Bourkes' reunion is quite significant though, considering that the siblings stayed away from each other and from their 'place of birth' for a long time. The story begins with Vaughn's arrival in Zimbabwe, after over two decades of studying and living in South Africa and Australia, respectively. Angela had lived on the farm up to the mid-1980s and then 'left for Britain, where ... she found huge fame and fortune as a wildlife painter' (Lang 2006:15). Angus, who had been living and working on the family's farm, was forced to relocate with his wife Jenny and two daughters Jessica and Lauren to a Bulawayo suburb in 2002 because of the violent disturbances that had been orchestrated on the farm by armed war veterans who had invaded the farm. It is evident, after the reunion, that the siblings' connection to the farm has been undermined by their absence from it. Vaughn thus describes to us the suffered displaced psyche, as 'this limbo. Always between places' (Lang 2006:5). Thus the novelist clearly describes the complex anxieties that white characters, produced from the colonial Rhodesian project, have to grapple with. Vaughn confesses to the existence of this split identity, as noted here:

> I have existed between identities. Between being Australian and what amounts to a ghost nationality. [...] Zimbabwe is given as my country of birth. I don't know why this inaccuracy troubles me. [...] But the fact remains: I was not born in Zimbabwe. I know nothing of what it means to be Zimbabwean. The real country of my birth, Rhodesia, no longer exists. This simple fact has, in one way or another, been the source of existential angst for many like me. (Lang 2006:5)

Lang therefore uses Vaughn's interior monologue to depict, in a confessional mode, the deracination and sense of limbo that some of the white Zimbabweans experienced in this post-colonial situation.

Some white characters are described as suffering from a displaced psyche. Vaughn's upbringing in Rhodesia was a shielded one. He enjoyed a privileged and shielded life, typical of a colonial childhood upbringing that is similar to the one depicted in Godwin's (1996) *Mukiwa: A White Boy in Africa*. This consisted of a closed interaction between their family and other white commercial farmers, just as Davey Barker and his family's (Holding 2005), during social gatherings at Shangani and at the numerous barbecues that his parents used to host for their neighbours at their farm. This protected life engendered an element of naivety in Vaughn that is only ruptured when he travels to South Africa to study. Vaughn, unlike Davey who actually looks forward to completing his high school education so that he could join the war against the African nationalist fighters (Holding 2005), confesses that he only realised the injustices arising from Rhodesian colonialism when he was studying at a university in South Africa. He thus became a liberal student activist who loathed colonial and apartheid racial divisions. This, together with the murder of his parents by nationalist fighters, forced him to migrate to Australia where he acquired this double consciousness that is based on experiences from his childhood under colonialism and exile. This therefore reveals how an awareness that is located in both oppressive Rhodesian and exile-based liberal values on issues such as race and the land shaped Vaughn's conflicting social and psychological perceptions of the post-2000 Zimbabwean conditions.

Vaughn finds himself in a contradictory position owing to the existence of this divided historical and social consciousness. He recognises that his sense of self and history is tied to Rhodesia. At the same time, he realises that Rhodesian colonialism was unjust and that the land redistribution 'was not only inevitable, but historically just ... But the crooked and murderous way the invasions were conducted was not what [he] had in mind' (Lang 2006:17). This split in consciousness depicts fully the duality and divided loyalties that Vaughn and some white characters were grappling with in this Zimbabwe of the early 2000s. It also resonates with the polarised views that dominated the media narratives about the land invasions in Zimbabwe (Willems 2004a). Thus, it is ironic that despite the exposure to western liberal views and his starting a new life in Australia, he has not managed to discard the Rhodesian colonial identity and culture that was instilled in him when he was growing up. Vaughn still possesses a nostalgic loyalty to the Rhodesian colonial heritage as noted when he puts on his 'Rhodesia is Super floppy hat' (Lang 2006:110). In addition, his brother, Angus' mindset is still located in the Rhodesian time space. He proudly displays the Selous Scouts eagle tattooed on his shoulder' (Lang 2006:10). Angus also recounts, with a reverent tone, the memories of his stint with the same Selous Scouts, which was an elite Rhodesian military wing that became popular among white colonials due to its notoriety in curbing the nationalist military incursions and in infiltrating the nationalist organisations during the 1970s. This is of course an interesting narrative strand because, as discussed by Primorac (2007:439–442), the state's political narrative of the Third Chimurenga to regain the land linked the past and the future in a distorted way in an attempt to blur the sense of historical continuity and justify the land invasions. Hence, some of the represented white Zimbabweans, or those now in exile but still with connections to the country as their place of birth, are depicted as still grappling with this displaced consciousness and divided loyalties, whose negative impact in the redefinition of the Zimbabwean identities is never difficult to imagine.

The constitution of this sense of dislocation that is present in some white characters, such as Vaughn and Angus, hints at the need for a change in perception and loyalties within some white characters. One can thus postulate that despite the fact that the depicted post-2000 land invasions are characterised by chaos and invoke anxieties within most white characters, the ironies inherent in the narrative style emblematise the need by some white Zimbabwean protagonists to move out of their own fragmented and imagined community where loyalties are still owed to the past Rhodesia.

This will enable them to become part of the collective African community, possibly join with the others in the fight against the Zanu-PF tyranny and strive for better social, political and economic conditions. This is suggested by the alliance between Angus and Saxon that was created in an effort to protect the farm and the fact that both were MDC activists. The views of Vaughn's South African-born colleague, who also resides in Australia, can be viewed as the pragmatic mindset that Lang seems to be suggesting as likely to reconstruct the whites' senses of self from their dislocated condition. The same mindset provides a strategic platform from which some of the represented whites can negotiate for their presence to be acknowledged in the re-imagining of what it means to be Zimbabwean and the redefinition of the rights to natural resources taking place in the form of the post-2000 land reforms. Vaughn recounts his colleague's views and thus highlights this need for the white characters to transform their views about the self and their mindset as shown here:

> He'd come to realise that the Africa he longed for was, in fact, Europe's Africa – not the sentimental umbilical fantasy that whites, like ourselves, had concocted in our hearts. What we really longed for, he said, was for the time when whites had a sense of hope and security, a time when they owned Africa. That time was gone forever, and the lost white tribe, now dispersed and dispossessed, was left in a contradictory limbo of moral awakening and existential regret. (Lang 2006:149)

The angst arising from identification with the past Rhodesian history and culture, while existing in the post-independent Zimbabwean time and space, compels Vaughn to be over-observant and detached like any ex-patriate or foreign observer of the post-2000 land invasions. Upon arrival, Vaughn notices the presence of the colonial past in the present, post-independent Zimbabwe. This is symbolised by the existence of colonial shops such as Meikles, Haddon and Sly and Solomon's Supermarket. He, however, later realises that this past culture has been gradually erased as he observes that the iconography of colonial triumph such as Rhodesian street names and the statue of the founder of Rhodesia, Cecil John Rhodes, were 'gone' (Lang 2006:7). He also notes that Bulawayo is replete with examples of structural, social and political neglect, which are all emblems of the social, economic and political decay that is evident in post-2000 Zimbabwe. Furthermore, there are ubiquitous signs of tyranny, as noted by the various portraits of President Mugabe at the airport. The erasure of the imperial and colonial cultural material, such as animal trophies, photographs of

Britain's Prince Philip and old Rhodesian prime ministers and the statue of Rhodes from the historic Bulawayo Club, which were replaced by the Zimbabwean president's photograph, are poignantly noticed by Vaughn. This therefore invokes anxieties in Vaughn, as he ponders at the social and political conditions defining this 'new' Zimbabwe.

These changes to and erasures of the colonial past lead to the constitution of anxieties within the larger white community in Lang's novel. The elderly Oom Jasper – who had lived and worked on his farm in the Shangani area until he lost his wife and the farm after an invasion by war veterans – is both bitter and obnoxious in his yearning for the lost colonial white privileges and sense of order. His bitterness at the social and economic downturn of this post-2000 Zimbabwe is understandable, as is his anger and trauma at the murder of his wife during the violent invasion of his farm. Worse still, his relocation from the farm to Bulawayo means a loss of income and impoverishment as their savings were being eroded by the astronomic rise of inflation in Zimbabwe, as was the case with other characters. Oom Jasper is thus rendered into vulnerability and psychological displacement. These constituted identities explain his diatribes about the post-2000 Zimbabwean political economy. For instance, Oom Jasper shouts grumblingly at a beggar in the streets of Bulawayo: 'Ask [for money from] your stupid president!' (Lang 2006:232). His outspoken racist views are noted in his fervent howling at the loss of the old order when 'the only way blacks gained entrance was as waiters, cooks or cleaners' (Lang 2006:230) and in his dismissal of all African leadership in comments such as ''n Kaffir bly 'n kaffir. Bloody bastards, all of them!' Similarly, Angus makes racist utterances in which blacks are 'munts', 'bastards' and 'kaffirs' out to destroy their white privileges, heritage and rights to the land. Lang thus captures these contradictions where whites appear as victims and yet still possess their racist identities that make up Zimbabwe's post-colonial condition in the twenty-first century, a condition noted by Pilossof (2009) as the 'unbearable whiteness of being'.

Lang, however, shows that the continued existence of racial perceptions and nostalgic identification with the old Rhodesian social and spatial divisions, by some whites such as Angus and Old Jasper, is not fixed. The constant quarrels between Angus and Vaughn over the post-2000 land invasions, racial politics and notions on belonging can be viewed as the narrative structure's indication of the writer's call for whites to engage in a dialogue that reflects on these crucial issues. These discussions must be frank but they are often brutal. This is noted in the tension and anger that characterises the arguments between Angus and Vaughn. For instance, in one such argument, Vaughn suggests, in an apparent naive tone that a voluntary displacement from the land could solve the post-2000 crisis and sooth the displaced psyches of people like Angus and Oom Jasper on the grounds that 'Africa needs to go back to the Africans. [...] Let them get on with whatever they have to do with it' (Lang 2006:179). Angus answers back stating that Vaughn should shut up and not 'give [him] that bloody crap about giving Africa back to the Africans' (Lang 2006:179). In addition, one also senses that as the characters discuss the various issues about the land invasions, this white community, and by extension the readers of this novel, are able to evaluate their position and options in an attempt to place themselves strategically and acquire complex qualities that will empower them to deal with these fluid perspectives and notions on the land, governance, race and national belonging in Zimbabwe. The plot shows that the Bourkes' active and rational engagement with their task of removing the remains of their ancestors and their witnessing of the conditions prevailing in the Shangani area force Vaughn and Angela to re-examine their identities and perceptions within the unfolding crisis. The author shows that the results can be bleak, but illuminating to the individuals involved. This is noted in Vaughn's realisation of the dual consciousness that defines who he is, while on a visit to the Matobo/Matopos Hills that:

> Despite the fact that I was born in Africa, I realise how *unAfrican* I am. Angela too. We will never be able to approach Africa without looking through the filtered lens of Europe – Angela with her artistic formulas invented and perfected by Europe, me with my need for a familiar historical edifice against which to see and measure the continent that bore me. (Lang 2006:149)

Moreover, the most pragmatic realisation that arises from these discussions and examination of the resultant contestations over land and belonging is portrayed in Angela's passionate assertion:

> 'For heaven's sake! You were born here, Vaughn! That makes you African. White African yes. Powerless in your place of birth – yes. But still African! I don't know why you make it so damn complicated!' [...]
>
> 'I'm sick of the whole idea of owning Africa. A more reverent view of our relationship to this continent is long overdue, don't you think? It's time we thought in terms of Africa owning us.' (Lang 2006:151)

Such perceptions indicate Lang's dismissal of the totalising perception pedalled by the Zanu-PF government that all white Zimbabweans are adamant and unrepentant racists who live and owe their loyalty to Rhodesia and the west. White characters, such as Vaughn, are described as constantly unpacking and challenging the remnants of colonial anxieties and loyalties existing within the represented white community. Furthermore, as indicated by the dialogue, there is a need for the constitution of this complex national imaginary that considers 'other ways of imagining collectives' as suggested by Raftopoulos (2003:234). This is probably most likely to result in the constitution of an all-encompassing definition of belonging and a hybrid identity that recognises the multiplicities in race, heritage and historical influences.

The land invasions impacted on the Bourkes in a number of ways. The impact of the land invasions on their personal lives is of great significance in this study. It is interesting that while the threats on the farm facilitated the Bourke siblings' reunion and a teasing out of issues on belonging and sense of self, their experiences during this period also engendered a process of memory-making. Nostalgia permeates through the Bourke's memory-making process especially as they relate to the idea of land, nation and belonging. Muponde and Primorac (2005:xx) note that most of the characters in white fiction such as Godwin's *Mukiwa* (1996) and Fuller's *Don't Let's Go to the Dogs Tonight* (2003) represent the experiences of white Zimbabweans as they recollect their upbringing and thoughts about the self, their marginalisation, suffering and belonging, and interaction with the landscape and the land. Similar thematic concerns are depicted here in Lang's novel. However, my focus is on the role played by the act of memory-making in linking the Bourke siblings with the land and belonging in the first few years of post-2000 Zimbabwe. Vaughn remembers the experiences of his first kill of an impala under the guidance of his uncle Rex, which though traumatic, was meant, according to the family tradition, to assist in moulding the typical Rhodesian male psyche in the nine-year-old boy. The memories thus recover a family culture and heritage that ties the white characters to the land and the Rhodesian identity, in a way similar to that of Chennells' (1982) and Pilossof's (2012) discussions. The siblings also remember the unforgettable relations they had with their late parents. Their mother, Nancy, would play the piano during special occasions such as barbeques with family and friends. Hence, the return to the farm triggers a process of memory-making that is not only nostalgic but inscribes the tragic and destabilising nature of the land invasions in that they signify the end of an era, family heritages and collective memories about land, in favour of the state's grand narrative about the land.

The recollections are also associated with the recovery of past traumas. Vaughn never knew the full details or circumstances surrounding his parents' death during the 1970s anti-colonial war in the then Rhodesia. The exhumation of their mother's remains therefore becomes a metaphoric journey, where 'digging up the past' (Lang 2006:99) leads to the siblings' recovery and coming to terms with the memories about their parents and the other ancestors. Angela confesses that 'I still miss them. The way they were. Such a bloody waste' (Lang 2006:171). All this registers their profound sense of admiration for their ancestors and the trauma they still felt over their parents' death. For Vaughn, digging up the graves becomes a process of healing in that the narrative's juxtaposition of the digging of the graves and his vivid remembrance of the description of how his parents died enables him to relate his memory with the actual place of burial. He comments thus: 'I see it, as I have seen it ever since, clear and distinct, as though I was there' (Lang 2006:172). Hence, the exhumations and the associated memory-making are depicted as cathartic for the traumatised siblings.

The digging up of the graves further enables the Bourke siblings to transcend their trauma and gain their peace of mind despite the ongoing chaos. The reburial of the ancestors at a Shangani church cemetery guarantees the honour and respect that they hold for them. It also safeguards their ancestors' physical presence and spiritual placing on the land that they lived on and loved, thus defying the ideological erasure and the intended displacement of whites from the land that the Zanu-PF campaigned for. The significance to the family of the reburial is presented in Angus' speech to the congregation on the day of the reburial, where he also notes that:

> Years ago, it seemed the right to rest in peace in the soil of our land was beyond question. What my family has gone through is what countless others have experienced already or are experiencing now. But this is our moment, and the time has come for us to mourn what this moment means for us. But it is also a time to remember and celebrate the lives of my forbearers. To celebrate who they were and what they contributed to this community. I remember when I was a kid, Oom Jasper Gerber saying Shangani wouldn't be the same without the Bourkes. It filled me with pride then, and it fills me with pride now. It's nice to know we at least meant something to this community, just as the community meant everything to us. (Lang 2006:192)

The reburial leads to the recovery of an idealised reunion between the Bourkes and 'former neighbours: the Thorntons, Griegalls, Mapstones and Pringles. All pushed off the farms and now living somewhere' (Lang 2006:190).

However, the congregation at this memorial service is multiracial, indicating that the wider community has also come to pay respects to the Bourkes. This undermines the racially based ideological spatial and political divisions that the ruling Zanu-PF elite and the war veterans were propagating in their rhetoric during the land invasions.

Land and the Conflict between National and Personal Histories

The contestations over the land, the dislocating effects and the associated memory-making process, are closely related to the conflict between personal and national histories. As discussed, the state's singular historical narrative (Raftopoulos 2004) has been privatised by Zanu-PF (Muponde 2004: 191). It is at best patriotic, as noted in its definition of the land as a resource belonging to black Zimbabweans that must be jealously guarded to prevent any re-colonisation by Rhodesian whites, and the imperialist Western countries (Ranger 2005). Harris (2005:105) quotes one of President Mugabe's speeches in which he states that white commercial farmers did not belong in Zimbabwe but in Britain and therefore should relocate to England, and asserts that such statements 'often evoke the ways in which Zimbabwe's complex colonial history informs the politics of white ownership of land, and white belonging on the land'. This identification of whites with a foreign and Western location, also evident in Buckle (2000 and 2003) as discussed in Chapter 3 and Lamb (2006) as discussed in Chapter 5, is indicated further in Lang's description of how the war veterans told Vaughn to go back to Australia as he was, in their perspectives, not an authentic Zimbabwean. This confirms that the dominant Zanu-PF's post-2000 crafted history and perspectives about the land and citizenship competed with other minor histories and perceptions, such as personal, family and other accounts.

Lang depicts the angst of the Bourke siblings which emanates from the fear of losing the land and their historical link to the land because of the state's racially based grand narrative on the land. The land issue intersects with history. But then, for the Bourkes, just as with other farmers described in the novel, their besieged farm is also part of their history and a history that must be guarded as well. Vaughn's account of his family's history and how his great-grandfather was one of the pioneers who colonised the area after the 1897 Shona/Ndebele uprising, and established a farm, is significant for the family's history and in linking the family with the farm. For the Bourke siblings, the loss of Hopelands Farm will be an enormous tragedy in that their physical and spiritual link to the land in the form of their ownership of and access to the ancestors' graves will have been erased from the place and history of the Shangani area. Vaughn is thus restless:

> I don't know Ange. This whole business is affecting me more than I imagined. I shut out the past all these years. Now I just can't escape it. Losing the farm ... I know it's inevitable – I'm resigned to the fact – but it's as though we're losing the last tangible remnant of our togetherness. As though the farm itself is a grave we won't ever be able to visit again. Only we can't exhume it and take it somewhere else. (Lang 2006:134)

The fact that the family is anxious to rebury their ancestors' remains signifies that family histories must be acknowledged and made to complement national histories. More importantly, the search for a solution to the land imbalances in post-colonial Zimbabwe, legitimate as they are, should be sensitive to other entitlements to the land and not seek to replace old dominations with new supremacies.

The novel posits that there are other histories that contribute to the formation of Zimbabwe. There are family histories, as noted in the Bourkes' history, colonial as it may be, which include the long history of the building of the farmhouse; the relationship between Rex, the uncle, and their father; the reality of their uncle Rex and their father's different lifestyles and visions on farming, and the siblings' personal histories indicated through their memory of their childhood on the farm. Other historical events include the contribution made by the sibling's father during the Second World War and the subsequent erection of the personal historical monument, the Cross, on a hill on their farm, and Angus' involvement with the elite Selous Scouts during the Rhodesian bush war. This underscores the inscription of different histories, some of it unpleasant, in the country's trajectory. Some of these events hold minor but significant historical meanings that should not be erased as they contribute to the mapping of the larger post-colonial complexities defining the country. They also affirm the historical role that ordinary people have made in the shaping of the country's diverse history. Hence, the novel is clear in debunking the dominant historical discourse that is privatised by Zanu-PF (Muponde 2004) and underscores that the definition of Zimbabwean history, just as factors linking individuals to the land, are multiple and complex, rather than the limited discourse that the Zanu-PF elite is propagating.

Ironically though, the history about the anti-colonial war in Zimbabwe, as noted by Angus, is full of contradictions. Angus recollects instances of brutality towards women, children and the weak by the nationalist fighters. He even describes some of the divisions and treachery that were experienced during the liberation war, as noted in Saxon's capture while he was fighting as a Zimbabwe African National Liberation Army (Zanla) fighter until he decided to collaborate with Angus' Selous Scouts. Even the later alliance and loyalty between the two is based on this past historical secret where enemies once allied together. The same absurdity is noted in the contemporary historical events described in the novel where the bulk of the war veterans' credentials are questionable as most of them did not fight in the 1970s war of liberation. In addition, the 1980s are noted in the traumatised psyche of the Ndebele as a period of brutality owing to the Zanu-PF government's orchestration of the extermination of a huge number of Ndebele people in the name of ridding the country of dissident elements, as documented by Godwin (1996) in *Mukiwa*. Hence, Lang is also able to subvert the dominant and sanitised nationalist historical narrative that is propagated by the Zanu-PF, thus depicting some of the historical errors and contradictions and major historical moments, some of which are defined by Nyamunda (2014) as elements of Zimbabwe's shifting history, which guide the Zanu-PF-led re-imagining and redefinition of the land in post-2000 Zimbabwe.

Conclusion

The drama that unfolds in the novel invokes anxieties and disrupts the white characters' lives and at times leads to violent deaths. However, it is evident that existing conditions can engender possibilities for the re-evaluation of the self and relations between different racial and ethnic groups and connections to the nation as a whole. As noted in this chapter, there are historically-based social and spatial conditions that led to the introduction of divisions and tensions between the characters occupying the different racial, social and political sectors in Zimbabwe. Nevertheless, Lang's use of a confessional but detached tone assists in the development of a thread that examines the social, spatial and political changes that are unfolding. He unpacks the inner thoughts, fears and limitations of some of the white characters, especially those of Angus, as they relate to the Zanu-PF's redefinition of the perspectives on and ownership of the land and the national imaginary of the land and politics in post-2000 Zimbabwe. The novel is therefore gesturing towards the vision of a better nation that is constituted, no matter how violent and dislocating the process may be, after an establishment of complex perceptions of the self and a consideration of different views about ethnic and racial groupings. The solution to post-2000 Zimbabwe's social and economic crisis is associated with strategy and rationality, which we can notice, from the novel, as the needed element in the re-structuring of Zimbabwe's perceptions on belonging, citizenship and access to national resources.

It is clear from Vaughn's statements that the white characters, as in Buckle's memoirs and Lamb's narrative, have been subjected to social and psychological dislocations owing to the land invasions. Furthermore, the other spaces beyond the farm and the agricultural land, such as Bulawayo and the other domestic and social spaces, are also disrupted as a result of the ongoing land invasions. Vaughn is unsettled by the neglect of infrastructure in Bulawayo, just as Angus, Saxon and Oom Jasper make disparaging remarks about the post-2000 social, spatial and economic collapse felt in the whole country. But, Lang still depicts the unfolding experiences as offering moments for characters, especially whites and to some extent radical and politically charged black Zimbabweans, to engage in some deep re-evaluation of their perspectives of the land, belonging and social relations with other Zimbabweans. This would probably lead to the constitution of a complex but not fixed national imaginary that acknowledges the heterogeneity of the country's population and multiple ownership and perceptions about resources such as the land.

Divided Worlds
in *House of Stone*

The narratives about the land invasions that have been discussed so far focus mostly on the experiences of the white farmers as they reacted to the invasions and occupations of their farms. The presence of black perspectives has been incidental. As noted in Chapter 3, Buckle (2000), describes briefly how some of her black workers were forced to attend all-night meetings and some subjected to physical violence by the war veterans occupying her farm. However, little space is given for a penetrating narration of farmworkers' experiences during the invasions. We are not given an insight into the black farmworkers' interests and yearnings, especially when considering that they had no title to land, even though some had generational working links with the farms. Furthermore, some farmworkers originated from neighbouring countries that include Mozambique and Malawi, which complicates the issue of land and belonging. The Zanu-PF grand narrative about land excluded foreigners and whites, which makes the absence of an in-depth literary representation of the black farmworker's experiences a huge anomaly. There is indeed a need to examine the voices and experiences of black farmworkers, for they were just as displaced as the white farmers and in most cases they can be viewed as the silent and ignored victims of this land reform project, hence their condition echoes Hartnack's (2014:2) notion of the 'problematic representations and omissions' characterising the post-2000 Zimbabwean crisis.

Christina Lamb's *House of Stone: The True Story of a Family Divided in a War-Torn Zimbabwe* (2006), a mixture of fact and fiction written in the journalese narrative style, is an interesting text that juxtaposes the voice and perspectives of both a black farm domestic worker, Aquinata and a white farmer, Nigel Hough. The fact that the author is a journalist reporting for a European media house should be underscored from the outset. As noted in Buckle's memoirs, media representations of the land invasions were polarised, with state media being pro-land invasions, and private as well as Western media being severely critical of the invasions and fast track land reform (Willems 2004 a; Hartnack 2014). As a result, there is a need to evaluate the veracity of Lamb's text on the basis of these questions: Is Lamb presenting a balanced and non-biased representation of her subjects' experiences during the post-2000 land invasions? And to what extent is this a true reflection or a true story of Zimbabwe's experiences during this period?

Lamb's text is examined in this book because it attempts to represent two voices and two different perspectives, those of a black Zimbabwean domestic worker and those of a white Zimbabwean farmer. The text draws on Aquinata – also referred to as Aqui in the text – and Nigel Hough's different narratives about their life histories during the post-2000 period. Lamb represents both characters' experiences through a reportage style conflating fact and fiction that juxtaposes both real life characters' experiences and the existing different social and historical perspectives on land. The setting is ambitious, it covers the colonial and post-independent period experiences, as well as the different and particular characters' experiences from their own worlds and perspectives about history, land and belonging, until both worlds intersect when Aqui joins Nigel's farm as a domestic worker and both encounter the experiences related to the post-2000 land invasions. Both characters' experiences unravel within social and spatial dynamics perceived by Kalaora (2011:750) as constituted by the divisions created during the early colonial period that sought to separate, especially, the white farmers from the black colonised labourer. Thus, both Aqui and Nigel's narrations of their colonial and post-independence Zimbabwean experiences are crafted from different racial, gender, class and political positions, whose nature dates back to the history of Rhodesian social, historical and spatial mapping. This makes the study of this text significant because we are able to unpack the author's attempts, which are a mixed success, to portray the different personal voices and perspectives on the land invasions. The narrative style, in which the main protagonists' narrative voices are juxtaposed and complemented by the author's, proffers the characters' separate histories, the intersection of these histories and depicts how their impact in the national historical trajectories assists in the portrayal of the conditions that shape both characters' views and actions during the farm invasions. The personal histories locate both protagonists in different social and historical spaces. As a result, the novel confirms the centrality of history in the shaping of the ideological views, individual and social imaginary on the land and other social, political and economic sectors of Zimbabwe.

Thus, the task in this chapter is to examine whether Lamb is able to offer a complicated narrative that links personal, national and contemporary history in the representation of the two different characters' perspectives on the land issue. Raftopoulos' (2004) observation about how the simplistic and Manichean analysis of the history of colonialism in Zimbabwe being propagated by the dominant Zanu-PF ideological machinery is undermining the possibilities of a creative examination of the role of whites in shaping Zimbabwean identities becomes instructive. Also deserving attention is Raftopoulos' notion that the post-2000 Zanu-PF's racially based anti-Western rhetoric aimed at erasing the role played by white Zimbabweans in mapping the social and spatial geographies and perceptions of land in Zimbabwe. The discussion in this chapter also considers Hartnack's (2014:12) review of studies on white Zimbabweans' experiences, especially during the post-2000 crisis, which outlines a number of generalisations about the white farmers' experiences in these studies and concludes with a call for further studies on 'whiteness' and 'to be more attentive to the ways in which various discourses can cause certain voices, histories and complexities to be forgotten or erased, especially in times of ideological and physical conflict'. Hence, there is a need to examine the significance of the description of Aqui and Nigel's occupation of divided worlds, from where they constitute different historical imaginaries and memories, in the expansion of our understanding of the contestations emanating from the post-2000 land invasions.

However, there is a need, in consideration of Hartnack's (2014) call for a more nuanced study, to examine how the influence of class and racial perceptions existing in the world of Aqui and Nigel can be linked to the historical impact of the Rhodesian inscription of colonial boundaries. There is a way in which the text seems to be interrogating history in an effort to destabilise its continued divisive impact in contemporary Zimbabwe, which might have led to these violent contestations for access and belonging on land. Ideas by Noyes (1992) on the establishment of colonial spaces are considered. Noyes draws on the fictional representations of the colonial experiences occurring in the German colony of South-West Africa, to outline how the colonialists appropriated and dominated African spaces and divided them into various bordered spaces in order to differentiate one geographical node from another. These colonial divisions were new and ignored the previously existing pathways, perceptions and utility values ascribed to these spaces by the colonised. Even the presence of the colonised subject in these spaces is erased, as noted in the various forced evictions of indigenous Zimbabwean communities from the late 1890s to the 1960s, and as discussed in Chapter 2. Kalaora (2011:750–751) in consideration of the link between colonial violence and racialised spatial divisions notes that after 1923 the Rhodesian settlers established and maintained their domination and distinctiveness by creating boundaries between themselves and black labourers, villagers and other colonised subjects, more especially in the area of agriculture through the enactment of laws such as the 1930 Land Apportionment Act, which enabled white farmers to place the labourers in certain spaces and thus control the African labourers economically and socially. The colonised were thus separated from white spaces and set under strict surveillance to contain any possible movement and maintain them as a source of cheap labour for the colonial economy. This brings in Fanon's (1963:29–31) critical views that the colonially-created social and spatial divisions impacted severely on the psyche of the colonised subjects and transformed most of them into restless colonised subjects. Thus, while being aware of the historical marginalisation of the colonised subject, the intention in this chapter is to determine how these divisions and existing Fanonian anxieties contribute to the contemporary racially-based contestations for land. It is also interesting to note how the invasions and occupations of the white-owned commercial farms, which as noted by Kalaora (2011:751), disrupted the old boundaries and white control on the farms, impacted on white farmer and black farm labourer relations, in this case the Nigel-Aqui relationship and their outlook on how to solve the crisis happening on the farm and understand their sense of the self in such a riotous time.

The fragmented and marginalised conditions of the colonised subjects were worsened by the hegemonic European-based ideological discourses on race, religion and other social values that sought to entrench the colonisers' superiority. Loomba (2005:91–114) discusses some of the important beacons in the historical trajectories of colonial expansion and consolidation and highlights how these developments led to the establishment of racial and social stereotypes that defined a race, class and political power based on difference in the European dominated colonial and post-colonial spaces. These colonial discourses thus entrenched a Manichean world (Ashcroft, Griffiths and Tiffin 1995) characterised by binaries that valorised the coloniser as racially superior, while the colonised were defined as inferior and ultimately positioned the colonialists, especially settler farmers as entitled to exclusive spaces and fertile lands while the colonised were restricted to less fertile land and worse still rendered landless. Primorac (2006:67) outlines the existence of specific linkages between colonial social and spatial divisions occurring in colonial Zimbabwe by stating that '[t]he Rhodesian state ... manipulated space on behalf of the white minority'. This underscores the role of colonial Rhodesian discourses on race and power in the establishment of separate worlds and different social outlooks on critical issues such as land ownership (Kalaora 2011; Hartnack 2014). Moreover, these colonially induced ideological, social and physical boundaries determine the different worlds that both Aqui and Nigel occupy and the different perceptions that they acquired as they grow up and during their adult life in the post-independence period. Therefore, there is a need to examine how the different class and racial outlooks, whose historical trajectories are traceable to the era of colonial spatial ordering discussed by Noyes (1992) and Kalaora (2011), impact on the way both protagonists negotiate with the events unfolding during the land invasions and shape the different ways in which both define and redefine their perceptions on land and national belonging. Furthermore, we should determine whether Lamb is able to destabilise these colonial binaries in this text and offer a solution to the race, class and ideological divisions that suggests possibilities for a new Zimbabwe.

The text continues the trend, evident in all the texts under study in the book, of representing the disruptive nature of the farm invasions. Like the Buckles, the Houghs are disturbed by the violent intrusion of war veterans, the deaths of some of the farmers and the siege of their farm by war veterans until they are forced to vacate it. However, the depiction elicits research curiosity over the way in which the author's perspectives intersect with both Nigel and Aqui's own narratives and views on the same historical trajectories and experiences. As a result, the suitability of the narrative style, where the author's voice dominates the plot development, but incorporates narrations and perceptions of both protagonists, needs consideration. The question is whether this symbolises an attempt at disrupting the colonially-established binaries. The use of a style that privileges multiple perspectives in literature has, nevertheless, been subject to critical literary and sometimes ideological review.

Pertinent to this study are other critics' considerations on the use of multiple narratives in the representation of the contestations for land in post-colonial Zimbabwe. Bower's (2006) review of *House of Stone* is instructive here. His review begins with a disparaging dismissal of the suitability of the use of a quotation from Alan Paton's *Cry, the Beloved Country* (1948), as one of her novel's epigraphs. According to Bower, the quotation: 'I have one great fear in my heart – that one day when they are turned to loving they will find we are turned to hating', positions the theme of love as major in African literary productions. He nevertheless refers to the continent's literary history from the 1960s and uses observations thereof to dismiss the positioning of the theme of love as dominant in African literature. I am interested in the element of his review that categorises the text as simplistic and the product of the so-called parachute journalist-writer, who gets into an area, ignores the complexities defining the events under focus; writes his or her work, mostly for a foreign audience and then leaves. Bower, therefore, criticises Lamb's inability to sustain the use of different 'case histories' and her failure to provide penetrating perspectives on why characters behaved or acted the way they did – as especially noted in Aqui's initial betrayal of the Houghs.

The author's journalist identity and employee status with a Western media house, certainly invokes discomforts and uncertainties over the veracity of her work. One can agree with Bower that parachute journalism glosses over the complexities on the represented ground. Willem's (2004) discussion on the polarised nature of media representations about the post-2000 land invasions, where private and foreign media narratives portrayed the invasions in a largely negative way for various reasons, while state media created a positive picture, is instructive here. Lamb, as a foreign journalist, seems to have fitted in such a polarity and her sympathy lies with the Western audience that she wrote for. There is a way in which *House of Stone*, in its narrative structure that focuses on each protagonist separately is suggestive of a continuation of the binaries that should be destabilised in post-colonialism. Lamb still views the character's trajectories and constitution of perceptions about history and belonging on land and nation within each character's exclusive experiences. For example, Lamb invokes a positive image and heroic aura in her description of Nigel's privileged upbringing on a farm and his entrepreneurial showmanship that sees him travelling in different places including the UK and China. As a result, the narrative makes the reader admire Nigel and perceive his purchase of Kendor Farm as well-deserved. This however, as noted by Bower, is constructed through a representation that does not acknowledge, or as noted by Hartnack (2014:2) omits, the colonial legacy of skewed land tenure that still plagues this Zimbabwe. Various narratives from the discipline of history, such as Palmer (1977), Alexander, McGregor and Ranger (2000), Alexander (2007) and Nyamunda (2014), outline this long history of land dispossessions and their lasting dislocating effects on the psyche of the colonised Zimbabweans. There is nothing wrong with Nigel working hard to buy the farm, but by valorising his showmanship and depicting it as justifying his ownership of the farm, the text glosses over the latent colonial discourses and settler acquisitive culture that still play a role in Nigel's perceptions about this land that he owns. Furthermore, Aqui's story of growing up in poverty appears incidental and does not make any impact in the world of the landed white farmer. Her position is that of a stereotyped farmworker that is only useful as Nigel's farmstead domestic worker. The narrative tone also suggests that her experiences of growing up in rural colonial Zimbabwe and worldview about race and land are minor compared to Nigel's, which in a sense is a trivialisation of the role of history in the determination of the post-independence land tenure and the justifiable need for the skewed land tenure to be corrected, albeit in an organised and peaceful way.

A similar criticism of Lamb's literary and journalistic work is also rendered by Makunike (2008). In his Afrocentric criticism of Lamb's text, Makunike (2008) states that:

> Christina Lamb, a British journalist, has carved out a niche for herself as some sort of 'Zimbabwe expert,' supposedly brilliantly able to explain the intricacies of 'the Zimbabwe crisis' to her fellow Britons and Westerners.

Makunike's criticism shows one of the major concerns in post-colonial studies, which, as argued by critics such as Ashcroft, Griffiths and Tiffin (1995), is the desire to subvert the literary and cultural productions that represent experiences from non-Western countries from an imaginary that is located in and privileges the West's perspectives. The criticism is thus worthy because the writer is a western journalist who most probably comes into the Zimbabwean post-2000 situation with her own European-centred perceptions and is writing for a European audience. Makunike however should have acknowledged, to some extent, the conceptual difficulties that Lamb faced as a white woman and foreign British national, and hence her documentation of the Aqui's life history as an outsider would always be difficult. Spivak's (1995) discussion on the difficulties of translating the story of the marginalised, the subaltern subject, reminds us of the onerous task that Lamb faced in her representation of Aqui's experiences.

Nevertheless, this difficulty does not absolve Lamb from the narrative's lack of a creative destabilisation of the old colonial binaries, which it seems to entrench. The task, however, is to evaluate the appropriateness of the criticism laid above, especially an unpacking of the relevance of this post-colonial criticism of the continued dominance of white based discourses in the representations of African experiences for a western audience.

This chapter thus examines the nature and significance of Lamb's representation of Aqui and Nigel's multiple perceptions and life experiences on the rural communal and commercial farm land, respectively, from the colonial to the post-independent Zimbabwe, and especially during the land invasions and fast track land reform programme. Ideas outlined by Bower (2006) and Makunike (2008) in their reviews about Lamb's novel and the key theoretical ideas that focus on history, culture, race, class and belonging in relation to the land in Zimbabwe, guiding this whole study, which include Hammar and Raftopoulos (2003), Raftopoulos (2004), Ranger (2005), Muponde and Primorac (2005), Pilossof (2012) and Nyamunda (2014), are therefore considered. Ideas from post-colonial studies as postulated, specifically by Loomba (2005) and those on spatial representations by Fanon (1963), Noyes (1992) and Kalaora (2011) assist in the analysis of this novel.

Different 'Consciousnesses' and Multiple Perspectives on the Land

The different views about and experiences faced during the post-2000 land invasions are linked to the social class, racial and historical divisions that exist in the colonial and post-independent Zimbabwe under focus in the text. Lamb's narrative style metaphorically indicates the divided worlds that existed and how they lead to the subsequent development of different social and historical consciousness of land in both colonial and post-independent Zimbabwe. The chapters are structured in a narrative continuum that begins at 'Zhakata's Krall, 1970' and ends at 'Kendor Farm, August 2002'. This indicates the social and spatial temporality covering the colonial period in the 1970s up to the post-colonial period and specifically the year 2002, when most commercial white farms, including Nigel's Kendor Farm, were invaded and occupied by war veterans. The separated world, owing to racial, class and colonial geographic boundaries that characterise the represented colonial time space is illustrated from the outset in the novel. The protagonists are described as occupying different social and historical spaces as noted in the first two chapters. The experiences during the 1970s are represented as divided into African experiences at 'Zhakata's kraal' (Chapter 1) and white experiences at 'Riversdale Farm, Headlands, 1971' (Chapter 2). These divisions are stylistically imprinted in the novel from the outset and metaphorically illustrate the historical and social antecedents of the multiple and opposing perspectives about land in this Zimbabwe. They also, to a larger extent confirm those binary oppositions in existence in colonial Zimbabwe, such that when the writer continues to write in such Manichean style, she fails to destabilise this relational linkage between the black and white Zimbabwean worlds, which has been historically skewed in favour of white Rhodesians and later on white Zimbabweans.

The life experiences of both Aqui and Nigel are also described as divided owing to the impact of the colonially prescribed social and historical boundaries. The colonial space, as noted by Fanon (1963), Noyes (1992) and Kalaora (2011) is a dominated one and divided into various opposing geographical and ideological boundaries. The divisions prevented the colonised subject's attempt to cross over to the other spaces and as a result they could not easily escape from their marginalised spaces. These geographical and ideological boundaries are represented by nodes that include Riversdale, the white commercial farms, where Nigel grows up, and cities, including Umtali and Salisbury, where Nigel goes for his primary and high school education. Furthermore, the nodes were circumscribed from the black communal rural areas and townships in colonial Rhodesia. The main protagonists' narratives begin with an outline of this past socio-spatial fragmentation. This therefore implies that the antecedents of the opposing perceptions of the land can best be understood by looking back to Zimbabwe's history and the associated geographical and socio-economic separations.

The effects of these colonially established social and spatial divisions are still felt during the post-independence period, as the novel's narrative style proves. Freeman (2005:306–307) examines the opposing political and intellectual opinions focusing on the post-2000 land invasions in Zimbabwe and then acknowledges, in concurrence with Raftopoulos (2004) that the history and effects of Rhodesian colonialism have a bearing on the land invasions. Freeman also argues further that the history should not be simplified, as done with respect to the patriotic genre (Ranger 2005), but must rigorously interrogate the positive and negative events, divisions and myths associated with the anti-colonial war and the nationalist Zanu-PF government's political decisions and attitudes toward the opposition and minority groups, just as Hartnack (2014:12) calls for studies on white experiences in southern Africa to guard against erasures of 'certain voices, histories and complexities'. This will establish a comprehensive understanding of the role played by colonial and post-colonial social, spatial and political divisions in the instigation of the land invasions and fast track land reform programme. The question to ask here in relation to Lamb's text, is whether she is rigorously interrogating the divisive and other adverse effects of Rhodesian colonialism in an effort to understand better the nature of the post-2000 land invasions in Zimbabwe.

This past colonially divided world and its associated historical and social memories are represented by Lamb as alive in both characters' consciousnesses. The attempt here is not to simplify the complex historicity that should be considered, as rightly opinionated by Freeman (2005) and Hartnack (2014) but is guided by the novelistic historical trajectories and the represented social and spatial divisions portrayed by Lamb. Both protagonists' narratives of their life histories are presented as separate, with each presented in its own chapters, but juxtaposed. These narratives notably refer to personal and historical memories that are shaped by each one's race and social class. This is noted in Lamb's non-fictive description of Aqui's early life history in the impoverished and ever-dry Zhakata village near Enkeldoorn, now Chivhu. This representation of Aqui's childhood experiences, portrayed in the first chapter, 'Zhakata's Kraal, 1970' underscores the significant social and spatial divisions that existed in this colonial world. The representation, which also incorporates Aqui's own 'voicing', reflects the village as removed from the centres of the colonial project, which are the white man's farms, missions and cities. Aqui articulates this marginalisation of the colonised subject's communal spaces in her statement that: '[*w*]*hites didn't often venture into our Native Reserves'* (Lamb 2006:17). Furthermore, the depicted 'Native Reserve' has exhausted soils, depleted forests and is susceptible to continuous droughts, thus making the villagers vulnerable. The author even makes inter-textual references to history:

> Zhakata's was in one of the Native Reserves, communal lands into which blacks had been shunted when the whites came, and it was a desolate place, the surrounding trees all having been shorn of limbs for firewood. (Lamb 2006:2)

Nevertheless, the portrayal, though attempting to draw on the impact of colonial history on Aqui's world, is simplistic here, as rightly noted by

Bower's (2006) criticism of this text and hence seeking to satisfy the Western readership's stereotypes, as pointed out in Makunike's (2008) review of the text, for she makes reference to the wanton cutting down of tress for firewood as arising from the environmental insensitivity of Aqui's people. Yet a critical analysis of Aqui's upbringing vis-à-vis Zimbabwe's colonial history, would have pointed Lamb to the link that exists between the recounted condition of perpetual drought and hunger with the history of colonial dispossession, a condition echoing Zimunya's (1982) seminal idea of drought and hunger in Zimbabwean literature as a metaphor describing the impact of colonialism on the lives of the black colonised subjects.

The author also depicts the significance of the colonial social divisions and their effect on some of the colonised subjects' imaginings of the land. Lamb describes Aqui's experiences of poverty in an isolated rural upbringing. She, thus, shows a link between these divisions and the formation of a grand national memory and narrative about the land among the landless and poor rural black Zimbabweans. This is evident in both Lamb and Aqui's own words as noted here:

> She had never been to Chivhu where the whites had their farms but she had heard villagers say that the fields there had special machines for spraying water for times when the rains did not come, and long golden corn, not like the stunted brown stalks that grew in their fields and often withered away. *They told of cows fatter than huts and chickens that laid giant eggs. My father said that the bones of our ancestors and cattle were under those fields and one day we would get them back from the whites.* (Lamb 2006:9)

It is little wonder that throughout the novel, Aqui's consciousness, born of her colonial upbringing as the inferior and dispossessed rural other, compels her to yearn for a restoration of their social and economic pride through the possession of resources, such as land. Nevertheless, this yearning for a return to the fertile and expansive land where the represented villagers of Zhakata's ancestors are buried bears resonance with Fanon's (1963:30) notions on the anxieties of the colonised subject seeking to invade those wealthy spaces of the colonial masters. In addition, the aspirations are illustrative of that desire, by the oppressed, to imagine the commercial farms – the spatial symbols and signs of colonial domination – differently. The kind of consciousness that Aqui holds as she perceives the land, reflects the contestations that characterised the land-hungry black Zimbabweans' imaginings of both the colonial and post-colonial land question. We as readers can postulate that the predominance of an anti-white discourse in the Zanu-PF government's rhetoric on land reform and the various attacks and displacement of white commercial farmers during the land invasions and fast track land reform programme represented in this novel, can be linked to the existence of this restlessness and dispossessed condition and deep yearning by Aqui to redress the past colonial land imbalances and other associated social and economic injustices.

Similarly, Nigel's own historical and social inclination compels him to hold views about Zimbabwe's social history and perceptions on land that contrast with Aqui's. Unlike Aqui, Nigel's upbringing was at Headlands, '[w]here all the surrounding farms … were white owned' (Lamb 2006:29). This underscores, from the beginning, the significance of race in the establishment of divided worlds. It is little wonder then that Nigel's subsequent perceptions on the land and national belonging are guided by his privileged upbringing as a colonial white male. His father even took him on hunting excursions and he sometimes ventured with his white friends into the forests, accompanied by black boys, whose good animal tracking skills he needed. In addition, he would move around the farm with his father to monitor farmworkers and direct the various farming activities. He also had the advantage of drawing from a family experiential history of living and working hard on the land. His parents owned Riversdale Farm, in Headlands and both parents, Mary and John, had been raised on their parents' farms in Rhodesia and England, respectively. As a result, Nigel acquired a sensibility that defined owning and belonging on a farm as intrinsic in the constitution of a white commercial farmer identity in Lamb's colonial and post-colonial Zimbabwe. It is clear that this consciousness is tainted with racial prejudices as noted in Lamb and Nigel's views on the mentorship that he received from his farmer father, where black farmworkers were categorised as inferior 'munts' that were useful only as providers of hard labour:

> From a young age, Nigel would often trot round after his father to inspect the progress of the tobacco or maize. *I was soon aware that farming was extremely hard work and that without endless supervision the munts would do nothing.* (Lamb 2006:31)

This quotation and Nigel's other accounts of his experiences, typify how the whites constituted perceptions about land that were economically-based. The land is a social and economic space in Nigel's perception.

Socially, the white farmer is the boss and superior to the black farmworkers. Furthermore, Nigel's childhood experiences show that owning a farm and working on the land is expected as per his family's tradition. The ownership also defines his ties to the land and assists in the constitution of a typical colonial Rhodesian farmer. The farm is also defined as a business, thus depicting a consciousness described by Chan and Primorac (2004:66) as located in a 'discourse on land [that is] almost entirely founded on its economic usage'. Nigel also describes his experiences in China selling ostriches and how he uses the proceeds as capital to buy Kendor Farm. By the time the war veterans besiege Nigel's farm in May 2002, he has managed to transform the farm he had bought a few years back into a viable one producing cattle, ostriches, tobacco and maize products competitively. This is indicative of his settler farmer showmanship and perception of the land as a resource available to be harnessed for huge financial benefits. The author underscores this showmanship and depicts Nigel's justified belonging on the land by virtue of individual tenacity and property rights. Hence, she seems to be entrenching the Western discourses condemning the invasions as a violation of property rights without taking into consideration the claims of those who were dispossessed during colonialism.

It is little wonder that it becomes very difficult for Nigel to relocate from Kendor Farm when his farm is under siege from the war veterans and other farm occupiers later on in 2002. Lamb describes how he degenerates into a restless character. Nigel's psyche that perceived the farm as his home and a business venture is indeed destabilised by the war veterans' siege of the farm. This siege, as he is aware from the experiences of the other farmers in the same Wenimbi district and the rest of the represented country, would destabilise the social and economic order that he has internalised from his early childhood at Riversdale Farm. He is eventually displaced from Kendor Farm to a house at a nearby school where his wife teaches. Nigel's character thus confirms the tragic and vulnerable dispositions that were acquired by some white Zimbabweans in the post-2000 era.

The significance of Lamb's constant use of flashbacks, in the form of Nigel's narration of his life history and her commentary, which portray Nigel's different perspectives on personal and national history and the land question, should be evaluated. Past childhood experiences of farming, a free spirited interaction with the landscape at Riversdale Farm, hunting and swimming, and the various family excursions to the farmers' social gatherings at the Farmer's Club in the nearby town of Rusape are retrieved and narrated in a nostalgic tone. Nigel nostalgically avows: *'For young guys that kind of life is like a dream'* (Lamb 2006:29). This consciousness clearly extolled an order and values that are segregationist. For instance, young boys such as Nigel enjoyed a protected upbringing, as a white farmer's son and young master, as noted in the way his interaction with black servant's children is trivialised because as he admits *'they knew so little about blacks'* (Lamb 2006:30) except that they were a mere *'supporting cast'* (Lamb 2006:30). In addition, Nigel regarded fellow students who were black at Prince Edward High School with great racist distaste. He even yearned to complete his high school and turn eighteen so that he could join the Rhodesian army and participate in the anti-nationalist war that he believed was necessary to protect white rule. What makes this perception critical is that, as one reads the novel, one gets the sense that people like Nigel still recall these unjust social and spatial colonial imbalances with nostalgia. And the author's view on such a perception is clear, for she hardly criticises Nigel's views. Nevertheless, the contestations for the land and the tragic violence witnessed during the invasions can be viewed as inevitable, considering that old victims such as Aqui also passionately view the land as stolen from their ancestors and thus in urgent need of redistribution back to them.

Colonial and Post-colonial Land Divisions and Violence in the Post-2000 Land Invasions

Just like Lang's *Place of Birth*, Lamb's *House of Stone* is written in a confessional mode that is nevertheless contradictory. This assists in illustrating the existing complex social and ideological differences and their impact on the unfolding of the post-2000 land invasions. It is true that the confessional mode implies that Nigel has made strides or is on a journey where he can transform his colonial and white-based historical and social memories about land in post-colonial Zimbabwe. For instance, Lamb narrates the anxieties that characterise the world of some of the portrayed whites as they contemplate over their future after the 1980 Zanu-PF election victory. These white characters thought the attainment of a nationalist government would result in the introduction of radical policies that would nationalise the land and mark an end to their lifestyle. Nigel confesses this restlessness in a statement that describes some of the perceptions that whites held on the newly appointed Prime Minster Mugabe: *'To us he was the Marxist ogre who had sworn to exterminate all whites'* (Lamb 2006:109).

Furthermore, an adolescent Nigel specifically dislikes the post-independence transformation of their school, Prince Edward, from an exclusively white colonial school, into a multi-racial one. He loathes the idea of staying in the same student hostel, participating in sporting activities with blacks and being outsmarted academically by a black student. It shocks him to have to accept that black students could achieve better grades than whites like him. Even the other white farmers' fears that they would be displaced from the land owing to a possible nationalist government's introduction of a huge socialist land nationalisation programme, were set aside as narrated by Nigel that:

> They (the farmers who visited Mugabe in Salisbury shortly after his inauguration as the Prime Minster of Zimbabwe) were expecting this communist gangster and instead he seemed this reasonable guy and they were impressed (Lamb 2006:117).

Hence, the continued presence of past colonial settler sensibilities, in post-2000 Zimbabwe, shows those perceptions of land that the once colonised characters and the Zanu-PF black nationalist elite would perceive as reactionary and use as a justification for the land invasions.

In addition, the fact that Nigel openly confesses, in his reflections, to holding black characters as invisible, as discussed earlier when focussing on his childhood experiences on the farm, indicates that he has been undergoing some transformation. Nigel, in one incident, vividly describes how he always notices Aqui's ever-smiling face and good nature with the children, which acknowledges her existence and shows his progression towards bridging his white master world and that of the black homestead farm labourer. Even Lamb clearly documents in the text that Nigel and other white farmers acknowledge that there is a need for an organised land reform programme that would address the existing landownership imbalances. The most significant moments are those when Nigel and Aqui 'talk about the differences between blacks and whites' (Lamb 2006:237), and the latter's experiences during the 1970s war. Nigel actually confesses to his white guilt and admits that he could have been one of the perpetrators of the violence and other injustices against blacks. These conversations also lead to the formation of 'a local mixed-race discussion group looking at what each race thought about the other to try and promote understanding' (Lamb 2006:238). This formation of a discussion group is considered by Moyo (2001:326) as one of the 'positive implications for the current land occupations', in that 'the occupations have confronted bad past and present race relations by forcing intensive interaction and discussions between whites and blacks in different roles'.

Interestingly enough, this commendable agency marked the beginning of a social redefinition, during a period where the government's land reform and associated ideological rhetoric, is never given prominence in the text. Lamb seems to be more interested in depicting Nigel as a victim of a black nationalist war against white presence on Zimbabwean land. The text suggests that both protagonists', and by extension the white and black world's outlooks, are still far apart, although perhaps the distance is lessening. This indicates the existence of these divided consciousnesses, one that Lamb in her writing does not give narrative prominence as rightly noted by Bower (2006), yet this consciousness assists in the continuation of opposing views that probably explain why there are contestations for the land:

> It was quite funny. All the white guys said there is no industry among the blacks, they are lazy. Then all blacks said the whites are not industrious. I was incredulous. I said, 'How can you say that? We create all the business in this country, run the mines, grow the food.' They said, 'Yes, that's what you do, you create things, but you don't actually work, you just sit and watch and we do all the work. (Lamb 2006:238)

The author also paradoxically represents the same nuances of social divisions typical of the old colonial order. Aqui's stature is portrayed with the same old colonial image of that African domestic worker or labourer who will always be known by his or her first name only. Lamb, in her attempt at documenting the voice of the farmworkers, something that is missing in most of the texts under study, evidently represents Aqui as the inferior domestic other and at times glosses over her descriptions, through her authorial power. This is a typical class definition that is steeped in a colonial discourse of power that privileges a white master and probably draws on Darwin's notions on white evolutionary superiority over the inferior black and less evolving colonised subject. Hence, there is a paradox here in that despite Lamb's attempts to document the complexities of different perceptions of the land invasions, by incorporating the voice of the black farmworker, often marginalised in literary and journalistic narratives of the post-2000 land invasions, she ends up positioning that black farmworker, in the form of Aqui, as subservient and inferior, which is a stereotypical image that spurs the same land invasions under focus here and resonating with Makunike's (2008) criticism of Lamb's use of Western racial undertones in her book.

One can thus agree to some extent, with Makunike's (2008) views that the novel was written for the consumption of Western readers and perpetuates the same misrepresentations that the former colonised world has been fighting against in the field of post-colonial studies. The normalisation of the undignified stature of characters like Aqui, seems to confirm the kind of superiority complexes and perceptions that the intended audience were expected to witness. Perhaps this also explains why Lamb is quick to show, without any explanation, Aqui's collaboration with the war veterans who were invading the farm and later on her reverting back to being the Hough's saviour.

An analysis of the social and spatial experiences emanating from the intersection between the divided worlds is also pertinent to this discussion. Generally, when the two worlds meet, the experiences are characterised by gross racial prejudices and violent conflict. In the first instance, the analysis of the represented experiences and consciousness of Aqui and Nigel demonstrate that they occupied divided worlds during the colonial period and this compelled both characters to acquire sensibilities that led to their constitution of conflicting perceptions about the land issue and national belonging. These differences continued to shape the psyche of Aqui and Nigel in Lamb's novel in post-independence Zimbabwe, and influenced the events during the post-2000 farm invasions in Zimbabwe.

It is clear that Aqui's colonial and post-independence social and spatial awareness is influenced by her displacement and violence-ridden upbringing. Her childhood and adolescent experiences are restricted by the dominance of family poverty. Her father worked as a contract labourer for the commercial white farmers and therefore struggled to provide for the family. The situation is made worse by the impact of the past displacement of the entire Zhakata community from fertile lands onto an arid and drought-prone communal village owing to what Kalaora (2011:751) calls those geographical orderings arising from the Rhodesian colonial legislative enactments such as the 1930 Land Apportionment Act and the 1951 Native Land Husbandry Act. In fact, Aqui's interaction with family members and the community, especially her grandmother who is a spirit medium, makes her aware of their colonially induced vulnerability owing to the displacement onto the overcrowded and infertile Zhakata communal area. Her grandmother keeps the social and historical memory of land through oral history, where she recounts, as noted above, how their ancestors were violently displaced from the fertile lands around

Enkeldoorn and Daramombe Mission during the early period of settler Rhodesian colonialism. Lamb also records Aqui's voice in which she narrates Aqui's version of the past history of the BSAC's imperial encroachment, the colonisation of both Mashonaland and Matabeleland and the 1896-97 anti-colonial uprising, as received from her father and ingrained in her consciousness. This oral and community-held social memory is both a counter-narrative to the colonial narrative held by the likes of Nigel and a metaphor of the resistant angst and imaginary that lurks in the consciousness of the colonised and dispossessed black villagers. This accordingly marks the existence of an alternative view to the narratives and perceptions of the social and spatial divisions characterising Rhodesia.

In addition, the memory of violence, resonating with Alexander, McGregor and Ranger's (2000) outline of the impact of displacement of the Ndebele from Bulawayo to various semi-arid parts of Matabeleland and the Midlands provinces in colonial Zimbabwe and the other forms of displacements evident in the nation's history described by Nyamunda (2014) dominates Aqui's psyche. Aqui witnesses some incidences of colonial violence. She recounts a disturbing childhood memory of her drunk father's abuse of her mother, which is emblematic of the paradox of colonial violence where the violated and dehumanised colonised man also violates his family and other colonised subjects, as underlined in Dambudzo Marechera's (1978) metaphor of the cyclical impact of colonial violence in Rhodesia portrayed in the novella, *House of Hunger*. She also witnesses, during her childhood at Zhakata in the 1970s, the effects of a commercial farmer's murderous violence in which a local village woman, Priscilla, lost her night-watchman husband called Lovemore. He had been '[thrown] on a fire to burn' (Lamb 2006:16) after being found asleep on the job by the commercial farmer. The horrible death of Lovemore haunts Aqui for the rest of her life as noted by the author herself (Lamb 2006:17). Furthermore, she is raped by her black headmaster while at primary school. Although the incidents are, as noted by Bower (2006), not given much prominence in the novel, they nevertheless illustrate the dominant presence of violence perpetrated by the powerful and how an intersection of the two different worlds of the colonialist and the colonised is often marked by violence.

Even the violence characterising the 1970s anti-colonial war is pertinent in this discussion of the violence that arises when the two worlds intersect. Paradoxically, Aqui and the other villagers were at risk from both the nationalist fighters and the Rhodesian soldiers. The black nationalist fighters, especially those from Zanu-PF, who operated in most of the country's rural areas in the 1970s, would punish anyone suspected of collaborating with the Rhodesian army and other repressive apparatus. Young girls were also at risk of being violated by both the colonial and nationalist soldiers. This is evident in the incident in which Aqui was abused verbally and nearly sexually molested by a Rhodesian soldier. Aqui's family later decided to move her to Marondera, where she would be safe from possible sexual violations that were common during the nationalist fighters' all- night meetings (*pungwes*). These experiences are indicative of the violent experiential space occupied by Aqui and other colonised subjects, especially those in the rural areas where the anti-colonial war was raging. This definitely entrenched a consciousness of a subordinated subject who is imprisoned by a colonially induced violence, poverty and restlessness. Such a world is completely opposite to the one that Nigel occupied. Instead, Aqui's world engendered a restless consciousness that ended up developing into resistant imaginings that shape the agency she engages in later in her life. Her experiences of rural poverty and colonial injustices force her to actively recruit potential black nationalist fighters in Marondera during the 1970s and spur her activism as a political commissar of Zanu-PF during the post-independence era. This therefore proves that colonial violence acted as an impetus for the development of resistant and activist identities within some of the colonised characters.

The prevalence of prejudice and violence within both the perpetrator and the victim, the dominant and the oppressed, or the possessed and dispossessed, as Nigel and Aqui's multiple identities and experiences symbolise in the narrative, also contribute to the various contestations for the land in Lamb's text and even the violence characterising the country's experiences. Even the dominance of violence and unequal relationships in the separated worlds and personal lives of both Nigel and Aqui play a significant role in the positioning of violence in the conflict over land and national belonging in the post-2000 land invasions, a condition that is similar to Fanon's (1963) ideas that locate violence in the moments of colonial contact and colonisation that will logically result in the use of violence by the colonised and oppressed in the fight for decolonisation (in this case its use of violence to fight against residual Rhodesian land imbalances) expressed in the chapter 'Concerning Violence'. There is also a paradox in those white commercial farmers, such as Nigel Hough, who bought the farms and did not inherit them from pioneer settler ancestors, who may have some justifiable claims and rights to the land, just as the black Zimbabweans do not have rights to all the land, for not all the land was stolen from them. As a result, this paradox makes the grand narrative about the land unstable. This explains why Aqui and Nigel's narratives on land are different, and in opposition to each other. Hence, any attempts to realise the dream of land redistribution to land-hungry black peasants and workers (in the case of Aqui) and the expectation that owning the land meant that the famer had the right to cultivate the land (in the imaginary of Nigel), becomes associated with violence. Each party believes in its own narrative that is in opposition to the other and passionately defends space or intended space, as symbolised in the fights between the white farmers and the war veterans.

The imaginings of a divided land result in a disruptive land reform project. As noted in the novel, old class and historical consciousnesses end up determining the nature of the process of the redefinition of access to land and belonging. The fact that the social, spatial and ideological divisions defining multiple contestations for land can be traced back to Rhodesian colonialism, positions the land invasions as a historically justified project with resonances of Fanonian (1963) decolonisation politics. Hence, the redefinition of the ideological, social and political meanings of land that begins in 2000 in Zimbabwe also involves the destabilisation of the old master-servant divisions. It also provides unimaginable possibilities for some farmworkers, most of whom were, like Aqui, of peasant background, victims of past colonial and other societal violations, and still hungry for the return of the land to the people as had been stipulated in the propaganda campaigns during the nationalist fight against settler Rhodesian rule.

Furthermore, the possibilities offered by the land invasions facilitated the farmworkers' and war veterans' transportation into an imagined temporal space in which the social relations and land ownership patterns would be reversed. Aqui experiences a metamorphosis of identity when she crosses over from her quarters to Nigel's plush farm house and imagines that she will be the new landowner. Even though Aqui later changes her mind, the consciousness that she acquires in the moment of action, is instructive:

> Once Nigel had gone from the house and she was left alone with the squatters, Aqui began to wonder about seizing the farm for herself. As she had suspected, most of the invaders were not real war vets and some of them were starting to look up to her as a leader. *Why shouldn't I have it rather than Netsai? I had worked for the party all those years whereas these people had come from nowhere. I had signed the list requesting a farm.* (Lamb 2006:256)

The land invasions are here portrayed as engendering this angst and at the same time opening the world of possibilities for the once dispossessed characters such as Aqui. They are also accompanied by frenzied dispositions, as noted in the way the war veterans and some of Nigel's workers shout 'Whites out! Blacks in! Whites out! Blacks in!' (Lamb 2006:249) as they intimidate Nigel and his friend Pete, who were under siege in the farmhouse. This provides an insight into the land invasions' impact at the personal as well as the ideological and operational levels. It is these new orders or possibilities of new orders that probably explain why Nigel could not believe it when he saw Aqui dancing with the invading war veterans – a condition typical of what Kalaora (2011:752) calls the trauma and incomprehension characterising the white farmers' lives as they try to come to terms with the invasions and occupation of their farms. Makunike's (2008) criticism of Lamb's work for being biased towards the plight of the white commercial farmers, her failure to delve into the inner consciousness of the war veterans and her inability to consider the significance of the historical and social complexities at play, thus becomes significant. Lamb indeed describes the war veterans' experiences from a distance. She also portrays Aqui and the war veterans with little or no interiority, thus privileging the perceptions and experiences of the white farmers, such as Nigel.

Furthermore, if the experiences of the commercial farmers were fatefully developing towards a tragedy, a narrative thread identified as characteristic in the novel *House of Stone*, as postulated by Bower (2006), then without denying that the deaths of some of the farmers and the loss of Kendor are tragic events, one must not overlook the triumph of good, amidst the murder and chaos on the farms. Aqui's decision to save some of the Hough's property by hiding it in various rooms and later asking to take it from the invaded farm to the Houghs, is paradoxically instructive of this madness (Kalaora 2011:759) in which survivalist and mutually beneficial relations between white farmers and black farm occupiers, in Lamb's case a farm domestic worker, are created. This, more importantly, symbolises the good in humanity that still exists in Lamb's violence-ridden Zimbabwe. It therefore indicates that the narratives of the land invasions will always be unstable and difficult to understand, but they have the potential of establishing new social orders on the farms and new understandings between white farmers and black farmworkers and the nation's different races and ethnicities in ways that we have not yet appreciated.

Conclusion

The text adds value to the body of literature that represents the experiences that took place during the land invasions in Zimbabwe. The reportage, drawing on national and individual social history, and multiple narratives emanating from the omniscient narrator and the two protagonists, Aqui and Nigel, assists in setting a narrative departure from the other representations under study in this book. The text attempts, unlike the writings by the other white writers studied here, to portray the contestations for land from the different points of view of both the white commercial farmer and the black Zimbabwean farmworker. The success is however limited, but it is clear that both protagonists' different perceptions about land, its ownership and the politics of belonging contribute to the contestations for land that culminate in the post-2000 land invasions.

The author, however, depicts the divisions, dating back to colonialism, as having a bearing on the different and opposing perceptions of the land and the land invasions. Colonialism divided the social and spatial worlds of both Aqui and Nigel and as a result the colonial discourse on race and the imbalances of class and political power led to the development of totally different views about the land in both characters. Nevertheless, the text's use of the fragmented narrative style, where chapters alternate in their description of each protagonist's experiences, entrenches the old binary oppositions that the author could have destabilised. The author seems happy at merely depicting different senses of national and family history in relation to the land, where each justifies their own historiography, with Aqui's recognising their dispossession as resulting from colonial forced migration from ancestral lands, while Nigel's typical colonial historiography justifies the pre-colonial African communities' loss of land in the name of a civilising mission and for rational scientific and business prosperity.

The novel therefore shows the nature and impact of the land invasions. The invasion of Kendor Farm, as was the case in the other texts under study, certainly become tragic as noted in the various deaths and the transformation of the farming spaces into chaotic spaces. This probably happened, not because humanity moves toward the tragic, but because the social, political and spatial gaps in the divided worlds of the whites and blacks had not been reduced since the attainment of national independence in 1980. Although the invasions and occupations were politicised and unnecessarily violent, they should not be simplistically viewed as a war situation, as the sub-title sensationally suggests, where black

Zimbabweans waged a senseless war on propertied and hard-working white farmers. The violent nature of the invasions and the exclusionary state discourses about land should be condemned, just as the white commercial farmer's entitlement to land and insistence on living in their closed worlds where, as Nigel admitted, blacks were invisible, should also be condemned. However, it is perhaps the unexplainable return to moral uprightness, such as Aqui's after initially joining and entertaining the idea of becoming the new owner, which can be considered as the required pragmatic new consciousness and social relations that this society must strive for. This 'new consciousness' may lead to the establishment of a peaceful coexistence on the land, but as was the case with Houghs, this is achievable after some loss, compromises and forgiveness on both the white displaced commercial farmers and the land-hungry black Zimbabweans.

Vulnerable Identities and Child-parent Relations in *The Last Resort*

This chapter examines Douglas Rogers' depiction of the way the land invasions impacted on human relations and perceptions of the self and society in the memoir, *The Last Resort* (2009). The memoir has the story of the farm invasions as the main plot but nevertheless allows us to enter into the space of the personal and social experiences of the affected farmers. The memoir is clear in depicting how some of the farmers' human experiences were turned upside down by the land invasions. The Rogers family were rendered vulnerable. They were transported into a space of constant worry about the possibility that they would be the next victims of the land invasions and occupations for a long period from 2002 to 2008. It nevertheless allows us entry into the personal experiences between father and child, author and subject material, and in the process reveals the creative and redemptive identities that Douglas Rogers acquires during the distressing period of the farm invasions.

The memoir describes the actual experiences of the author's parents at their 'backpacker lodge [well known for] ... pizza night' (Rogers 2009:7), called Drifters, situated outside Mutare, as they struggle to prevent their eviction by the war veterans and supporters of the Zanu-PF party during the height of the land invasions and occupations of white-owned farms in Zimbabwe. Lyn Rogers, a retired lawyer, and his wife, Rosalind, meet with distressing circumstances as they await the invasion of their smallholding, which they claim was not suitable for any agricultural production. The

Rogers are portrayed suffering endless anxiety as they think about the day of their eviction since their farm has been published in the national newspapers as earmarked for compulsory acquisition by the government. Their vulnerability is worsened by the fact that the neighbouring white commercial farms in their valley have already been occupied and Drifters Lodge appears to be a sole island among the occupied farms. Drifters is thus cast as the last outpost of white landholding, hence the symbolic title '*The Last Resort*'.

In spite of these circumstances, Lyn develops a number of survival techniques, similar to those white-farmer-black-occupier relationships examined by Kalaora (2011) that were considered by some white Zimbabweans as a sign of madness. He establishes a cordial relationship with a nameless new chief of the valley who is Political Commissar for the new settlers of the former white-owned farms near Drifters, in order to get the Political Commissar's protection of the farm from possible invasion as well as to seek assistance in getting an audience with the 'Top Man', a chief minister close to President Mugabe, who has the ultimate power to save Drifters from the invasions. Lyn's other survivalist activities include the turning of the lodge into a brothel, growing marijuana for sale on the farm and opening up the lodge's bar and accommodation for rent to black and white Zimbabweans. The most significant result of Lyn's enterprising activities during this period is his renting of the lodge's bar and restaurant to a politically connected young male called Tendai, which results in the lodge and smallholding being protected from seizure right up until the end of the novel – after the 2008 parliamentary and presidential elections that brought in a government of national unity consisting of the MDC and the Zanu-PF elected members.

This chapter therefore discusses the specific personal experiences and perceptions of self that are depicted in this memoir. I am well aware, though, of the paradoxes noted in the way whites claim belonging in Zimbabwe through victimhood and a belonging based on placing oneself in that negotiated space between imaginaries of a nostalgic past and the excluding present, as discussed by Harris (2005). The chapter also analyses how the actual crisis moments and sense of victimhood impacted on parent-child relations within the Rogers family.

Personal narratives and life stories have generally been associated with the construction of various perceptions and the narrator's search for meaning as they remember or try to come to terms with past events. Personal narratives and life stories usually treat momentous events, which McAdams (2008:252) citing Singer and Salovey (1991) and Tomkins

(1979) describes as 'the high points, low points, turning points, and other emotionally charged events' in an author's life. I am interested in 'the low and turning points and emotionally charged events' within a life story for various reasons. First, these characteristics are evident in Douglas Rogers' memoir; his is a narrative about the distress and emotional turmoil suffered by both the author and his parents owing to the government's land reform programme which took a sudden and radical shift after 2000 and turned the spaces of white commercial farms into turbulence. Second, the white farmer individualities and perceptions of their positions constructed during these moments significantly map the position of white farmers and their families during the contestation for belonging and allow the reader to witness the social turmoil suffered and the turning points that emerged during the encountered distress. This is evident in the way the author's parents had to redefine their own relationships and those with their neighbouring farmers and tenants at Drifters Lodge.

Life narratives are sometimes used for redemptive purposes. In a redemptive story, the narrator is encouraged, especially in the field of psychology, to narrate about negative events encountered in the past in an effort to compel them to make narrative sense, find meaning in the suffering and in the process move on with their lives (McAdams 2008:253–254). The crisis moments, 'the low points' and 'turning points', also considered as the moments of transition in one's lifespan, for which personal narratives are best recognised (Singer 2004; Bauer and McAdams 2004), are quite significant in that they enable us as readers to determine the transformative identities emanating from the encountered crises and transitions. Thus, since, 'life transitions – not even the voluntary ones – leave the individual with a strengthened sense of meaning or happiness in life' (Bauer and McAdams 2004:574) it becomes pertinent that we examine whether the crisis and its turning points impacted positively on the personalities and relationship between Lyn and Rosalind Douglas and their son, and that between the Rogers family and their neighbours as well as how they relate with the Zimbabwe body politic.

The chapter's focus is two pronged. First it seeks to examine the shifting personhoods and perceptions by the farmers, as especially noted in Lyn, as they go through the trajectories associated with the politics and practices characteristic of the farm invasions and land reform programme. Second, it analyses the ways in which the post-2000 crisis condition and its destabilisation of the notion of white belonging on land by ownership (Harris 2005) lead to the construction of creative strategies and strengthened relationships between family members and other members of the depicted society. Thus, the analysis is based on the premise that the crisis transports some of the affected farmers into contradictory spaces, where they are on one level victims, but could also transcend this vulnerability and acquire strategic and survivalist qualities. It also postulates that the land invasions, farm occupations and ultimate fast track land reform programme compelled the characters to embark on new ways of looking at and relating with family and other members of society. The chapter argues that family relations, especially father-son relations were transported into the realm of enhanced connectedness, and secondly, just as survivalist qualities were formed, new strategic relations, crossing over race, class and sometimes political affiliations were also formed thus indicating a new image of the nation and the human condition constituted out of this crisis.

White Farmer Vulnerabilities and the Construction of Survivalist Qualities

News of the impending farm invasion of Drifters invoked anxieties and vulnerabilities within the Rogers family. This condition of anxiety and vulnerability is similar to that experienced by other white farmers and their families, such as the Buckles, Bourkes and Houghs as noted in the analyses in Chapters 3, 4 and 5 respectively. What makes the impending invasion of Drifters interesting and probably absurd in the author's perspective, is his naivety that the farm's leaning, through the backpacker lodges, towards tourism would spare it from invasion and the fast track land redistribution programme. This view is however dented by a nameless white farmer who gave Douglas a lift to his parents' lodge Drifters and in the conversation between the two, expressed the lurking white farmer vulnerability:

'Where are you going?' he asked.

'Outside Mutare, a place called Drifters,' I told him.

'Drifters? The backpacker lodge that had the pizza night?'

I did a double take. […]

'Are your folks still on their place?' he asked with a hint of surprise.

'Ja, so far. It's not really agricultural land. Accommodation mostly, a tourism business, the backpacker lodge. They should be alright.'

He looked at me like I was deluded, touched by the sun.

'I wouldn't be sure about that, my friend.' (Rogers 2009:7)

The author's recollection and inclusion of this conversation in the early stages of the memoir is significant. It pits the state of instability that farmers were now in, 'a state of being never sure' and the existence still of a belief that reason would prevail as noted in Rogers' belief that the lodge would be spared because 'It's not really agricultural land' (Rogers 2009:7). The nameless white farmer's cynicism thus debunks the rationality of the programme. It also underscores how white farmers were transformed into vulnerability: ownership was no longer guaranteed and as such their lives were punctuated by restlessness and anxiety, symbolised in the quoted scene by the nameless farmer's chain-smoking, as they contemplate the inevitable appropriation of their farms every day.

The memoir invokes an apocalyptic image for the white farmers as is evident in most of the white narratives under discussion; however, the apocalyptic trope is most prominent in Buckle's (2009) representation of Meryl's diary about the rescuing of abandoned animals as discussed in Chapter 7. The Rogers' livelihood as white landholders is depicted as being under huge threat, for judging from the way the invasions were taking place in their valley they were next and worse still their tourism project had ground to a halt. The Rogers are hence transformed into restless and vulnerable characters.

The text, however, goes on further to exhibit the qualities of a redemptive story in that both the narrator and the family members search for 'positive meanings in [their] negative events' (McAdam 2008: 255). Lyn does not let the constant threat of invasion of their smallholding and lodge dampen his spirits or reduce him into a sense of stasis. First, Lyn opens up relations with a Zanu-PF Political Commissar in charge of the resettled black farmers on the valley. Here, Lyn's resilience and scheming abilities, contrary to the notion of white farmer madness observed by Kalaora (2011) as held by some white Zimbabweans, are depicted in that he creates a relationship of convenience with the Commissar. He sought, from the relationship, access to talk directly with the minister in charge of land resettlement, dubbed the 'Top Man', a chance to plead his case that the farm was not suitable for agriculture and as such should be removed from the list of farms gazetted for compulsory acquisition. Later on, Lyn offers the Commissar lifts into town, at a time when the country is reeling under a huge shortage of fuel and basic commodities. As a result, the Commissar promises to turn a blind eye to events such as his giving refuge to displaced white farmers, turning the farm into a marijuana farm and sub-letting the bar to Tendai, who in turn provides accommodation at Drifters for prostitutes and illegal diamond dealers who were striking it rich in Mutare after the discovery of diamonds at Chiadzwa outside the city.

In 2007 Douglas Rogers himself also establishes a strategic relationship with a war veteran and soldier in the Zimbabwean army, Sergeant Walter Sebenza, who facilitates a meeting between Piet de Klerk and the Top Man. The meeting results in De Klerk getting back his cattle which had been looted during the invasion of his Kondozi Farm. This relationship, apart from introducing the political story through Walter's narrative about his war of liberation experiences in the valley and the nearby city of Mutare, and that of his ancestor's colonial displacement from the valley, strategically leads to the acquisition of protection for the Rogers. Rogers expresses his family's fears of losing Drifters to Walter, who makes the commitment: 'Don't worry, Rogers junior. I will protect your mother and father' (Rogers 2009:236). Lyn is able to meet the Top Man and plead his case, although the meeting never yields any definite result. Nevertheless, Walter comes to the Rogers' rescue later on in the text. First, he makes sure that Lyn is not targeted by the Zanu-PF machinery for supporting the opposition MDC party. The realisation by Lyn of the fruits of this strategic relationship are gut wrenching as described in a chance encounter that Lyn has with Walter on the Mutare –Harare road:

> They pulled over on opposite sides of the road and stood facing each other for a minute as a couple of cars clattered past. Then the soldier bounded over.
>
> 'Mr Rogers,' he boomed, patting Dad on the back. 'Good to see you again!'
>
> 'Hello, Walter,' said dad, less enthusiastically. 'Good to see you.'
>
> The soldier looked exhilarated. His eyes were alive. My father had never seen him so happy before.
>
> 'I saved you, you know,' said the soldier.
>
> 'What's that, Walter?'
>
> 'I saved you.'
>
> 'What do you mean, saved me?'

'Your name came up in a security meeting. They said you were MDC.'

My father's stomach twisted into a knot. He felt an involuntary smile come to his face. (Rogers 2009:288)

Second, the eventual invasion of the farm on 21 June 2008 was foiled by Tendai, the tenant operating Drifters' restaurant business, who calls Brigadier Gatsi in command of the nearby Mutare military base to scare away the invading war veterans and thus save the farm. What is interesting is that the connection between Tendai and the brigadier was facilitated by Walter while he was renting a cottage at Drifters. In all these cases the Rogers demonstrate their tenacious efforts in seeking to keep the farm. Furthermore, a story of these experiences is indicative of the redemptive self (McAdam 2008:255); this time a story of survival and emancipation from the jaws of politically motivated land dispossession. Hence, the Rogers were able to turn their negative experiences into positive ones and craft tenacious and survivalist strategies that were aimed at a continued survival and belonging on the land.

Douglas Rogers assumes a narrative personality resonating with McAdams (2008) notion of personal stories as constituting qualities that are based on the search for meaning and an understanding of past terrible times. Rogers' narrative personality is constituted in the representation of his family and other white commercial farmers' experiences. His story attempts at understanding his aged parents' experiences and views as they try to save their land. The narrative also inflects the personal with the political story as the author seeks further an understanding of the rationale behind the land invasions. As a result, we also encounter the Rogers' experiences on land and other stories about the pre-colonial displacement of black Zimbabweans from the valley. Rogers thus juxtaposes the historical narrative with that of his family's buying of the land and their showmanship in turning the unproductive farm into a fledging tourism smallholding.

Also accompanying the Rogers' story on the farm are the individual stories of the refugee white farmers such as the De Klerks, Herrers and Hamiltons. These white farmers' narratives, which describe each farmer's particular experiences of arriving in the farming region, indicate the farmers' mythical Rhodesian showmanship (Chennells 1982) and ultimate establishment of successful farming ventures in and around Mutare. For example, Charlotte Kok, occupying Cottage 14, describes how her parents migrated from South Africa after the Anglo-Boer War and bought a farm at Rusape in 1929. She later marries Basie Kok, a rugby player from South

Africa in the 1950s, and both husband and wife establish a prosperous tobacco farm in Nyazura, outside Mutare. Furthermore, Piet de Klerk, a former Springbok and Rhodesian rugby player displaced into Cottage 6, 'had come to Rhodesia from Cape Town in 1953, bought the farm in 1968 and originally grew tobacco and raised cattle' (Rogers 2009:107). De Klerk had worked hard to encourage the government to construct the Osborne dam, which then supplied water for their world-class Kondozi Farm and the whole of the Mutare region. Kondozi produced vegetables for different European markets with the assistance of out-growers from the surrounding villages, who had been trained by Piet's son, an agronomist. Interestingly, Rogers juxtaposes narratives by the Political Commissar and Walter, the former war veteran and army sergeant who is a tenant at Drifters who describes how his ancestors were displaced under chief Zimunya during colonialism, with that of his family's reeling under threat of displacement and the trauma experienced by the resident refugee white farmers. As a result, the author depicts the competing narratives about land that constitute the political context to the memoir and the story about the invasions.

Rogers' narrative is nevertheless limited in its portrayal of the complexities about Zimbabwe's land issue. It fails to give more weight to the story about black displacement from the land. The memoir structurally gives more attention to the white farmers' experiences and limited narrative space to the Commissar and Walter. While the nature of a memoir or life story is that the narrator's story takes prominence, the fact that the sub-title states that it is a memoir of Zimbabwe, demands that we be given balanced perspectives and that considerable attention be paid to the black narratives about the invasions and farm occupations. Furthermore, the text entrenches some of the colonial discourses that led to the rise of the inward black nationalist discourses that labelled all white farmers as racists deserving to be uprooted from the land and Zimbabwe. First, the text draws on and extends the old Rhodesian settler and pioneer myths in its description of the refugee white farmer experiences, which is indicative of some colonial and racist nuances that led to these invasions. Second, Walter is described in beastly imagery and associated with a typical colonial mapping of the black other as a beastly and inferior subject:

> Mom was right. The soldier was built like a buffalo: a full-grown bison with flared nostrils, skin as dark as hide leather, and enormous bovine eyes that were glassy black holes, set so far back in his head that it was

impossible to tell what colour they were. His large head was shaved bald and was as smooth as polished soapstone carving. But he had a kind moon face that was innocent as a child's and he was surprisingly quick with a smile, despite his dead eyes. (Rogers 2009:230)

This narrative to some extent still entrenches the same old white stereotypes that post-colonial Zimbabwe should disrupt in order to achieve a balanced heterogeneous sense of belonging and memory about land. Rogers' redemptive self serves as a way of seeking creative belonging to the land and a connectedness to the Zimbabwean nation. Nevertheless, the story fails in a big way to acknowledge the diverse narratives about land. Instead, there are genuine and historical stories about past black displacement from the land owned or seized from the white commercial farmers that should be recognised, without condoning the violence and chaotic nature of the post-2000 land redistribution programme.

The Rogers' ability to constitute the positive out of their unsettling experiences is also noted in their endearing welcoming of white and black tenants on their farm during this period. Drifters offered lodging to displaced white commercial farmers, such as Piet de Klerk, who lost his highly productive Kondozi Farm in the Odzi farming region outside Mutare. The presence of these displaced white farmers underscores the white commercial farmers' narrative of victimhood and their constituted victimhood. As noted by Harris (2005), the perceived victimhood held by displaced farmers made them believe that they had suffered enough to claim belonging in Zimbabwe. The narrator's comment that some of the displaced farmers 'simply [stayed] because this was *home*. They were Zimbabweans. There was nowhere else to go' (Rogers 2009:91), attests to this notion of belonging through victimhood prevalent in white Zimbabwean imaginings that is also noted by Hartnack (2014). The presence of these white farmers also serves as a critical exposé of the supposedly irrational and chaotic nature of the land invasions. Most of the farmers, as already pointed out, are portrayed as farmers who arrived in the Odzi farming region and surrounding valleys with nothing, but with determination rose to become successful tobacco, cattle, vegetable and other produce farmers. As a result, these white farmers' narratives assist in the authors' mapping of the post-2000 land invasions and fast track land redistribution programme as defying logic considering that some of the displaced farmers, such as Piet de Klerk, contributed greatly to both the national economy and the local communities' survival. Some displaced black farmers and tenants, such as the enterprising young man, Tendai, who was operating the bar and restaurant on a lease, were also resident at Drifters. The farm here becomes a metaphor of the kind of cross-racial and multi-class community that Zimbabwe needed.

Lyn also becomes an active member of the opposition MDC, an indication that the Rogers are committed to shaping the future of Zimbabwe. The MDC is a black-dominated party and by joining it Lyn plunges himself into national politics and braves the associated risk of retaliation from the ruling party, which was well-known for its brutal attacks on the opposition. This risk is confirmed later on when Walter informs Lyn about the planned Zanu-PF attack on Drifters that he had thwarted. Credit should also be given to the Rogers family, especially Lyn, for constructing new ways of relating with fellow farmers and other black Zimbabweans and allowing this 'united nation' to settle on their farm. This interracial community established at Drifters illustrates the pragmatic qualities and perceptions that the Rogers acquired as the crisis unfolded.

Remapping Parent-child Relations in Times of Crisis

The land invasions shaped or transformed the parent-child relations in the memoir that is under focus here. The white narratives about the land invasions already discussed reveal that the family unit was subjected to huge distress during the social dislocation often witnessed during the invasions and occupations. An examination of how these events impacted on the white farmers' interaction between themselves becomes pertinent. Hence, this section examines the impact of the land invasions and occupations on the parent-child relationship in Rogers' memoir. The intention is to extend the idea of the redemptive self by testing the nature of the parent-child relations that were established during the crisis moments and as such determine if these child-parent relations, assumed to have yielded further connectedness, can be considered as a positive story arising out of the representations of the land invasions.

The memoir begins with an exposé of a dislocated relationship between Rogers and his parents. From the beginning of the novel, the narrator's migrant and writer status is established as significant to the portrayal of the way the land invasions would impact on the parent-child relationship, especially the father-son relationship in the memoir. Rogers has been away in London trying to establish his career in journalism such that on his return he realises: 'I am a foreigner in my own country' (Rogers 2009:4). We can also assume that exile must have affected the degree of closeness between the author and his parents. His frantic call in 2000 to check on his parents' safety as the violent invasions intensified, which was dismissed by Rosalind and Lyn Rogers as something not to worry about, shows that he was out of touch with his parents' lives. The author's identity as a journalist facilitates his return home and enables him to get reacquainted with his parents. Rogers was tasked by the London bureau of the *Daily Telegraph* with writing newspaper articles about the invasions and farm occupations. Later on he decided to write his story and that of his parents during this period. His story, the memoir, becomes more of a story about re-establishing connectedness between child and parents in times of crisis, as noted in the first dinner after Douglas' return:

> My mother had made oxtail stew, my favourite dish, and Dad opened a bottle of Pinotage. We sat at the antique yellowwood table in the dining room and talked late into the night. Or rather, they talked, I listened. They were letting go, a catharsis; they needed someone who would listen. (Rogers 2009:17)

This quotation shows how his relationship with both parents was renewed, with food and wine enabling the jovial re-bonding. In addition, the rest of the memoir gives more prominence to the experiences that Lyn went through, which in a way illustrates the way the personal story of the author becomes entwined with that of his father thus establishing a narrative connectedness between parent and child.

The narrative indeed gives prominence to the recovery of a close parent-child relationship. The memoir describes the author's growth and gradual comprehension of his father's tenacity during the crisis. Rogers returns to Zimbabwe in 2003 'to tell my parents it was time to go' (Rogers 2009:40), because he is probably reeling from an outsiders' perspective that lacked a better understanding of his parents' experiences. He nevertheless depicts how the crisis facilitated his physical reunion and narrative way of reconnecting with his parents:

> *The Daily Telegraph* had assigned me to write about my parents, these *bittereinders*, the last of a dying breed. There were now fewer than a thousand farmers left on their lands, and twelve had been murdered. The invasions had only intensified since the 2002 election. (Rogers 2009:40)

Although he flies back to Zimbabwe and is reunited with his parents, it is mainly the act of writing about his parents' lives that establishes a creative means through which Rogers gets to understand further the impact of the crisis on his parents. He also gets to understand his parents' perspectives on the land invasions, occupations and associated politics, as well as the strategies they used to save their farm from seizure. It is thus interesting to note that the author describes later on, in a light humour that exudes admiration, how his father established a strategic relationship with political players such as the Commissar, Walter and the well-connected and enterprising Tendai who rents Drifters restaurant and bar. The tone of parent admiration begins to dominate Rogers' narrativisation of his father and mother's strategies to save the farm as aptly noted in the description of the way the new tenant Tendai brought Drifters back to life:

> My parents looked on in wonder. Drifters had not been this busy since the millennium – and that seemed about a thousand years ago. As for Tendai, they now saw him in an entirely new light. [...]
>
> But who were my parents to wonder? Drifters had miraculously re-invented itself gain. And their chalet business, their main source of income, was thriving once more. (Rogers 2009:246–247)

The author's depiction of the parents' lives as they dealt with adversity indicates the son's transition from fear and negativity, shown in the first chapter, where Rogers makes a call to find out if his parents are safe, to a creatively positive tone that affirms his parents' tenacity. The memoir can thus be considered as a narrative of writing the self on a journey into bonding with his father and mother in times of crisis.

The author and his parents continue, despite the ongoing crisis, to maintain constant contact. These contacts and reunions enable further social and restorative connections between child and parents. Even though Rogers returns to London and then relocates to the United States of America to stay with his fiancé, he never loses touch with his parents. Rogers describes how he would constantly call his parents, especially his father, on Skype in order to keep in touch. He even includes his invitation to his parents to attend his wedding held in the United States of America in this life story. The wedding thus facilitates those momentous experiences in a person's life story, which also take place even in crisis contexts and end up enhancing the relationship between the author and his parents. The wedding week 'had been a whirlwind week' (Rogers 2009:120) and was quite significant in the author and his parents' social life. It connects Rogers and his new family with his parents and friends. The feasting and conversations held during the wedding week are also an affirmation of life and the continuation of an ideal existence as individuals, families, business people and nation that the memoir laments as lost in the world of the Rogers and other white commercial farmers in Zimbabwe.

The memoir also depicts Lyn's transformation into a father figure during this period of the land invasions. As already noted, the negativity of the invasions and occupations lead to a creative understanding by the author of the complexity of the land invasions and also enables his connection and appreciation of his parent's lives and ideals. Ultimately, the memoir celebrates his parents' tenacity in keeping their land and their ability to rise beyond the adversity suffered during the represented period. The memoir, however, describes the way in which the crisis enables Lyn to acquire a flexibility that transforms him into a father-figure for his new tenants through the cordial relations he develops with them. Lyn's relationship with Tendai, the politically connected young man who rented his restaurant, best describes this positive metamorphosis of his from a nuclear family head to be the father-figure of other people. That the relationship between Lyn and Tendai is a warm one is evident in the friendly tenor that is always kept between the two: Tendai always greeted Lyn as 'Mr Rog' and the latter called Tendai 'Mr Cool', which is indicative of the relaxed and close relationship between the two. Thus, if sons are there to save their parents in times of crisis, then Tendai's arrival to save the Rogers from the forced eviction by a group of war veterans is emblematic of these symbolic father-son relations that Lyn entered into during the crisis.

Lyn's entrance into opposition politics, as a member of the MDC, also enabled him to interact and assume a father-figure status among some of the political activists. The political activism is the turning point which enables him to work with MDC politicians such as Brian James, a son of an old white farmer in Mutare, who was later elected Mayor of the city in 2008. Lyn also assists two young MDC activists, Pishai Muchauraya and Prosper Mutseyami, who were being hunted by the Zanu-PF in the 2008 elections in which the MDC won a parliamentary majority. The father-figure quality in Lyn is aptly depicted in the way he finds a suit for Pishai to wear on his first day in Parliament. While the act resonates with the notion of white paternalism, dating back to what Kalaora (2011: 750–751) called a farmer benevolence seeking to maintain a colonialist social order on the farm, the fact that Lyn risks his life keeping these activists on his farm and giving them a dignified send-off into the realm of public politics is emblematic of the transition moment in his life where he now accepts other blacks as equals. This also reflects the constitution of Lyn's character which possesses the qualities to transform some of the devastating effects of the land invasions into positive victories.

Hence, Lyn's choice to ignore the racially based exclusions imposed by the Zanu-PF to work with and 'father' the young opposition activists, is one such redemptive element associated with the narrative about the land invasions' impact on the lives of some white commercial farmers.

Conclusion

The memoir underscores that there are various positives arising out of this personal story, set in crisis moments and pitting a white landholder against a dominant black nationalist state, black against white and neighbour against neighbour, as well as dislocating those considered as non-citizens and enemies of the state. These positives are noted in the character transformation and acquisition of survivalist identities, as noted in Lyn's initiatives that enable him and his wife to survive during the grim economic meltdown that Zimbabwe went through between 2002 and 2008 and to save his farm from invasion. An additional positive development arising out of the tumultuous conditions is the underscoring of possibilities for the establishment of cordial relations between enemies. Lyn establishes strategic relations with the Political Commissar and Walter, where the latter even saved Lyn from the Zanu-PF post-2008 presidential election violence against supporters of the opposition MDC. These established connections and character metamorphoses can be viewed as the emblem of the kind of vision that post-2000 Zimbabwe needed – one based on tolerance, attempts at understanding one another and constituting new and unexpected relations, such as that between Lyn and Sergeant Walter Sebenza, to build a better society.

The Crisis, Animals and Activism in *Innocent Victims*

Throughout time, society has learnt to live harmoniously with its animals, especially pets and other domesticated animals. A harmonious relationship with animals and the landscape enables a certain balance between humanity and nature and is especially godly in Christian imagery. Thus any attempt to disrupt the balance can be viewed as retrogressive, horrible and an unwarranted evil. This chapter continues to draw on Alexander's (2007:183) key statement underlining the land's role in the constitution of, among other issues, senses of self (identities), memories, social and historical struggles, as well as being a muse of literary imaginations. It however, extends this notion by examining representations of the land invasions and occupations in relation to human-animal interactions and the ecology on the affected farms. Chapter 2, among other issues, discusses the growth of colonial discourses on the Zimbabwean environment and landscapes. Ranger's (2000) examination of the BSAC's establishment of the national parks and conservancies in the Matopos area outlines the history behind the growth of contesting views in the imagining and use of the environment and landscapes between the colonial settlers and the local Banyubi communities, where one was European, colonial and scientifically-based and the other African and social-culturally-based, respectively. On an interesting note, Hughes' (2010) study, though aptly criticised by Pilossof (2014:138–139) for being simplistic in its evaluation of how white settlers established a sense of connectedness with the

Rhodesia landscape, underscores, rightly so, the significance of settler emotional attachment with the colonial rural landscapes at the expense of the environmentally-indifferent local black communities. Thus, both historians, (Ranger and Hughes) highlight the centrality of environmental and ecological concerns in the discourses about land, history and belonging in Zimbabwe; a centrality that I also consider in this chapter where I analyse the impact of the invasions on the animals held on the farms and in the conservancies.

What is also interesting is that the narratives studied so far also employ the motif of white commercial farmer despondency over the ecological destabilisations occurring on the farms during the land invasions. Buckle's (2000) memoir, examined in Chapter 3, describes how the farm invaders, in transforming themselves into the new settlers, randomly cut down trees, cleared off forests and hunted wild animals. Lang's *Place of Birth* (2006), discussed in Chapter 4, portrays the Bourke siblings' close attachment to the animals and its landscape. It is thus evident that environmental and ecological concerns feature prominently in the construction of perceptions, and social and historical memories in Zimbabwe. This demands that we also analyse some of the post-2000 white writings pitting land invasions against the environment and ecological set-up on the farms. It is important that we examine the nature of ecological and human-animal relationships during the invasions. Under focus here is the displacement of farmers and farmworkers from the farms, the restructuring of farming spaces and the abandonment of domestic and wild farm animals and how that determines the constitution of perceptions of the self, everyday experiences and belonging and access to farms and farm work, as well as the ultimate post-colonial image of the nation based on the way animals and farms are treated during the invasions and occupations.

This chapter examines Buckle's *Innocent Victims: Rescuing the Stranded Animals of Zimbabwe's Farm Invasions – Meryl Harrison's Extraordinary Story* (2009), a literary diarisation of Meryl Harrison's activities as an officer with Zimbabwe's Society for the Prevention of Cruelty to Animals (SPCA). The chapter explores the depiction of Meryl's character qualities and experiences from 2000 to 2004. The experiences recorded are drawn from Meryl's vivid diary as she travels around Zimbabwe to rescue animals that were left stranded, distressed or came under threat during the various land invasions and the construction of new settlements and tenure patterns in Zimbabwe's different farming and conservancy regions. The chapter also evaluates the social and political significance of Harrison's documentation of the lived experiences and the author's commentary in mapping the post-2000 ideological and historical trajectories and notions on belonging and citizenship in Zimbabwe. The intention here is to explore how the land invasions, remapping and new settlements on the farms impacted on the human-animal relations and the ecological conditions on the farms. The fact that we are examining the narratives from a human-animal nexus using an ecological lens assists us in broadening our views about the representations and enormity of the post-2000 land invasions in Zimbabwe.

Considering the Diary Motif, Ecocriticism and Ecology

Buckle's (2009) text draws on Meryl Harrison's diary entries from March 2000 to December 2004. The text describes Meryl's everyday experiences and activities as an animal protection officer of the SPCA in Zimbabwe. This period is marked by land invasions and settlement on white-owned farms mainly by the veterans of Zimbabwe's war of liberation, Zanu-PF supporters and other ordinary Zimbabweans. The major consequences of these invasions and occupations included the displacement of the farm owners, their families and most black farmworkers, as well as the subjection of the farmers' animals to distress and abandonment. The highlights of Meryl's experiences during this period include rescuing dogs, cats and other pets, as well as commercial dairy and beef herds and game left stranded on occupied farms. These rescued pets were saved from the stressful and life-threatening conditions in various farming regions such as Bindura, Chinhoyi, Bulawayo, Harare, Mutare and Chiredzi. The animals were either re-united with their owners, adopted by new owners, or sometimes euthanased. These events are vividly documented by Meryl in her diary and Buckle's literary representations of such activities. The text also reconstructs Meryl's true life experiences as she organises programmes to save wild animals which were stranded, and as she was threatened by poachers or made vulnerable owing to the breakdown of conservancy programmes and the destruction of game parks in areas such as the Bubiana Conservancy.

Buckle's re-writing of Meryl's experiences, from a literary perspective, demands that we examine the nexus between the diary and representations of inner personal views in times of crisis. The diary genre plays a significant role in the representation of private and personal experiences, especially in times of crisis. A diary represents the documentation of the personal everyday experiences and also expresses the diarist's inner and intimate perceptions on these experiences, sometimes in a spontaneous and raw way (Bolger, Davis and Eshkol 2003:580). It has over the years become a significant literary genre which is associated with women's uncensored writings about their private experiences and intimate thoughts about personal relations and sometimes their bodies (Podnicks 2000:3–6). The literary diary is also known for its documentation of everyday experiences during crisis times as aptly shown in the popular holocaust diaries, such as *The Diary of Ann Frank* (Brenner 2003:1–5). By drawing on a diarist's documented everyday lived experiences, the literary diary locates itself within the body of life writings that incorporate the autobiographical and fictional reconstruction of the diarist's experiences (Podnicks 2000:5), whether in private spaces or during crisis moments.

I am interested in the literary diary as an invention of the autobiographical acts of the protagonist's agency, as especially noted by Podnicks (2000) in her discussion on how women in general and prominent literary women such as Virginia Woolf in particular, used the diary to write about their own experiences and thus surpass the existing censorship. Also pertinent here is the association of the literary diary with crises, especially the text's depiction of the protagonist's everyday and intimate handling of terror or crises. Brenner (2003:5–7) shows this in her examination of holocaust diaries as a testimony of resistance to terror. Thus, it is interesting to see how Buckle and Meryl, both women, use the diary motif to confront the everyday horrible experiences encountered on the farms, and evaluate the heroism and agencies in their activities, one fictively recreating Meryl's experiences and thoughts, and the other documenting activities as she moves around Zimbabwe rescuing stranded and vulnerable animals on the invaded and occupied farms and conservancies.

The literary diary's drawing on the diarist's private experiences enables the constitution of an intimate relationship between the reader and protagonist as well as identification with the protagonist's subject formation in particular distressing conditions. As readers, we get drawn to the diarist due to their direct voice to us, and we are forced to admire the protagonist as the representations are generally presumed to be drawing from the protagonist's genuine life experiences. The literary diary, in this case, becomes some form of resistant life writing that 'affirm[s] individuality and personhood under the rule of terror' (Brenner 2003:5). Furthermore, the documented experiences and their representations also speak back to the hegemonic forces or perpetrators of the distressing conditions, thus linking the literary diary with post-colonial literature's focus on resistance and speaking back to those in power. The task at hand here is double: the first being to evaluate the represented subjectivity of Meryl as she rescues the abandoned animals and provide a vivid and supposedly authentic documentation of the violence, destruction and disruptions taking place on the farms and conservancies that she visited between April 2000 and December 2004. The second task examines both Meryl and Buckle's mapping of Zimbabwe's ecological conditions in relation to the radical and black nationalist social, historical and economic trajectories that were pitted against the residual white colonial and Western discourses on social and economic development, during the early 2000s.

The nexus between ownership and land use patterns, notions on the landscape (ecology) and historical belonging and identification with land is, as noted in Chapter 2, a source of contestation and motive for various social and political agencies. There is a need, however, to consider perceptions on landscapes and ecological concerns and to examine their impact on human-animal and environment relations and notions on belonging. The farm, as noted so far in the analysis of the previous narratives, is transformed into a space where the opposition between nationalist Zanu-PF discourses about the anti-Euro-American imperialism project are pitted against white farmer and residual colonial, as well as Western perceptions on access, use and control of natural resources, such as land and the flora and fauna on it. What is interesting is that, while Huggan and Tiffin (2010:2) postulate that there is a need to 'bring post-colonial and ecological issues together as a means to challenge continuing imperialist modes of social and environmental dominance', the post-2000 land invasions in Zimbabwe, however, disrupt this conventional convergence. This is because white farmers and the text's protagonist's activities in rescuing the animals, assist in representing white commercial farmer dismay at the disruption of their farming activities and the accompanying ecological turmoil taking place on the invaded and occupied farms. However, lurking in the background is the fact that the dismay points to the disruption of old colonial and white farmer social and economic dominance over Zimbabwean resources. Furthermore, there is a reversal in that the new and dominating views about the farms, and their animals and landscape, are located within the nationalist discourses of the war veterans and other participants in the land reform programme. We are thus compelled to examine how we can perceive a situation where the former colonised introduce their own discourses and practices on the occupied farms and rise to replace the former social and ecological order in their interaction with both the environment and animals on the farm. Hence, theoretical concepts drawing on post-colonial ecocriticism become pertinent here. Huggan and Tiffin's (2010:4–17) ideas, particularly those on the presence of environmental racism in the West's perceptions about the way the former colonised or indigenous societies interact with their environment, and their call for the recognition of the contribution of the environment and animals in the development of humanity as well as that of the need to employ post-colonial ecocriticism in order to speak against a force or a group of people that dominates the environment, animals and society, are indeed critical in my examination of the land invasions and their impact on the environment and human animal relations.

It must be pointed out that there exists a body of non-literary narratives, mostly academic and journalistic, which examine the nexus between the post-2000 land invasions and the resultant environmental damage and poaching of wild game and forests. Most of the journalistic narratives about the impact of the land invasions and occupations by new black farmers are marked by apocalyptic images, typical of the concept of an environmental apocalypse (Huggan and Tiffin 2010:51). These narratives document rampant poaching of conservancies, national parks and occupied white-owned farms by the beneficiaries of the fast track land reform programme.

Groenewald (2002a) in the *Mail and Guardian* describes the war veterans' destructive occupation of Richard Pascal's game farm. After occupation, they prevented him from providing water to his 30 black rhinos, resulting in the death of one during the occupation. Eventually, they forced the well-known white farmer conservationist to leave his farm by April 2002. Groenewald (2002b) later paints a horrific picture of the ecological disaster culminating from the land invasions and farm occupations by stating that 60% of wildlife on Zimbabwe's private game farms and conservancies were destroyed in the first two years of the government-supported radical land restructuring project.

Further reference is made to the disruptive effects emanating from the poachers and new settlers activities on conservancies. Conservancies such as Bubiana (IPS 2007), Save Valley, Chiredzi River and Gonarezhou National Parks (Commercial Farmers Union Report 2011), are described as marked by conditions where 'the rule of law has collapsed and the environmental destruction is reaching epidemic proportions'. The poaching is also depicted as impacting on the country's tourism and conservancy projects in a huge and negative way, thus, associating Zimbabwe's post-2000 land invasions, occupations and fast track land reform programme with the image of an ecological Armageddon. The tone of these journalese texts map the land invasions and fast track land reform programme as a return to 'primitivity' or a rabid violation of the

Western ideologies of development (Huggan and Tiffin 2010:27). This resonates with the view that the establishment of national parks by the BSAC and Rhodes implicitly marked an introduction of colonial social and scientific advancement in the colony's ecological sectors (Ranger 1999b), thus confirming this journalistic image of how the post-2000 Zimbabwe land invasions and land reform were emblematic of a social and ecological regression.

The reportage was also broadcast in the international media and the new media, thus positioning itself for global consumption. Its accessibility by international readers and unlimited circulation on the internet and through the new media means that these narratives about the ecological crisis unfolding in the space of the invaded and occupied farms and conservancies acquired an activist streak. The white farmers and the threatened conservancy projects were now portrayed as spaces occupied by vulnerable and victimised animals and humans. To write about their condition was to make the world notice and condemn the unfolding ecological atrocities. This, therefore, brings in the dynamic of post-colonial ecological activism. Huggan and Tiffin (2010) describe post-colonial ecological activism as including the literary exposure of conflicts emanating from an intersection of different forms of advocacy. Both critics state the exposure as including 'examining the social, cultural and political factors at play in the eviction of local (indigenous) people from the nature reserves and wildlife parks' and 'seen as an interventionist or even activist enterprise, along the lines of Robert Young's shorthand definition of post-colonialism as 'a politics and philosophy of activism that contests the disparity [between Western and non-Western cultures], and so continues in a new way the anti-colonial struggles of the past' (Huggan and Tiffin 2010:14).

However, the tenor of activism evident in the depictions of the ecological concerns about the post-2000 Zimbabwe land invasions and farm occupations is complex. First, it is the white farmer, associated with the historical memory of Rhodesian colonialism (although some farmers, as Buckle attests in her memoirs in Chapter 3, were never beneficiaries of the past colonial project) who is subjected to nationalist and hegemonic state interventionism on the site of the farm. This is unlike a criticism based on the experiences of the ordinary citizen, as discussed in Roy's 'Greater Common Good' (1999), in which the Indian government is criticised for initiating the displacement of ordinary citizens in the Namada Valley to construct a dam. Second, the activism seems to be against the abuse of the environment and disruption of the white farmer-animal and environment relationship owing to the land invasions and farm occupations by the war veterans and supporters of the Zanu-PF government. Third, the reportage and literary writings are in most cases targeting international audiences thus focusing global attention on the Zimbabwean situation. This complicates the eco-critical mapping of the land invasions and farm occupations in that it disrupts the traditional view of ecocriticism's activism. The criticism evinced here is focused on the Zimbabwean inward and exclusionary land redistribution programme and its impact on the traditionally privileged white farmers' experiences on the land and their relationship with the ecology, and not the historically burdened former colonised black Zimbabweans.

Furthermore, the activists' empathy with white commercial farmers and their criticism of the decimation of wild and domestic animals and the environment, appears to justify the nationalist Zimbabwean government's narrative about the need to fight Euro-American imperialism. This is because the tenor of the activism's targeting of an international audience and hence condemnation of the state's programme, and the resultant EU and USA's introduction of targeted sanctions against the government elite, as a way of registering the West's disapproval of the project, maps the Zimbabwean government officials and the radical project on land reform as victims of the Euro-American hegemonic agenda. However, as noted by Huggan and Tiffin (2010:14), the task of a post-colonial ecocritic is to show awareness of the nuances of conflict 'when different forms of advocacy are brought together'.

This chapter, thus, examines the nature and significance of the different discourses, namely the white farmer and the protagonist Meryl's discourses and the nationalist grand narrative about the land. These competing discourses are significant in mapping the power relations between local and international sensibilities and power politics and how they are being destabilised in relation to the ownership and access to the farms, human- animal relations and the constitution of perceptions of the self and on belonging in this tumultuous post-2000 Zimbabwe.

Human-animal Interactions and the Ecology on the Invaded Farms

The land invasions and occupations had a sudden and long drawn-out impact on the rhythm of life on the farms and the survival of both wild and domestic animals on the targeted farms and conservancies. This section examines the impact of the invasion and occupation of white-owned farms on the relationship between people, plants and animals, the ecology (Shikha 2011:1) and on the conservancies and game parks in different parts of Zimbabwe. This enables us to determine the post-colonial trajectories and power-relations being constructed in the radical re-mapping of the nation's access and ownership of land and its plant and animal resources. The ecological crisis manifesting itself in places such as the Chinhoyi, Bindura, Karoi and Mutepatepa farming regions in the Mashonaland West province; the Bubiana Conservancy in Matabeleland South; and other prominent farms, such as Charleswood Estate in Chimanimani, Chipesa Farm and Waltondale Farm in Marondera, are depicted by Buckle through her literary representation of Meryl's diary entries of her experiences as she rescues animals that had been abandoned in these different ecological spaces.

The text pronounces, from the beginning, the advocacy element, typical of post-colonial ecocriticism's 'writing wrongs' trope (Huggan and Tiffin 2010:16). It makes society aware of the human actions that were damaging the environment and more specifically human interactions with animals with the objective of seeking ways to handle the ethical quandary and restore ecological balance (Shikha 2011:2-3). Buckle introduces Meryl as a dedicated wife and, and above that, Chief Inspector of Zimbabwe's SPCA, whose commitment is noted in her countrywide travels to treat, rescue and protect animals. Nevertheless, the advent of the land invasions and occupation of white-owned farms and conservancies complicates Meryl's work:

> Meryl tried to be prepared for any eventuality but rescuing animals from invaded farms was uncharted territory: it had never been done before, by anyone, anywhere in the world. (Buckle 2009:4)

As a result, the land invasions and their associated ecological crises initiate character and personality transformation in Meryl which also results in her entrance into the larger space and discursive performance of national and global animal rescue and ecological restoration advocacy. This transformation into a globally recognised animal rights activist, which is triggered by the first rescue of a Great Dane puppy called Black Jacques that had been 'beaten repeatedly by thugs armed with sticks, stones and bricks' (Buckle 2009:1) at a farm outside Bulawayo, is aptly noted here:

> Meryl didn't know in July that, for the next five years, virtually every day of her life and every aspect of her job would concentrate almost entirely

on rescuing animals from seized and invaded farms. Her family, friends and personal life would all take second place as she worked tirelessly to do the right thing for animals who had become the innocent victims stranded in the midst of the mayhem. Meryl was compassionate, fair and responded well to a challenge and for the animals of Zimbabwe these qualities were to be their saving grace because the abnormal had become the normal in Zimbabwe, and would stay that way for some years. (Buckle 2009:12)

Meryl's travels around Zimbabwe during the period 2000 to 2004 enabled her to enter the farms affected by land invasions and occupations. Her mission was to rescue pets, domestic and wild animals that had been abandoned on most of these farms after the forced displacement of the mostly white farm owners. Meryl's diary, thus, threads the different farming regions, such the Chinhoyi-Bindura-Karoi-Mutepatepa and Norton-Harare-Ruwa-Goromonzi-Marondera and Mutare- Chimanimani areas, whose state of turmoil and accompanying ecological crisis she vividly describes from her personal witnessing.

For instance, Meryl's visit to Two Tree Hill Farm in Chinhoyi, during the first week of August 2001 is represented by Buckle using religious imagery and apocalyptic images. First, the chapter describing the rescue of the dog Nandi, begins with a religious epigraph, (there are many such epigraphs in the text) a verse from Exodus 20 verse 17 that speaks against greediness and coveting a neighbour's wife or workers. This and other invasions documented in the text are thus associated with images of an evil return to an ungodly life. The chapter is, therefore, punctuated by a modernist tone, typical of the First World critical sense of God having abandoned his people. Meryl describes what she witnesses 'as the face of evil' (Buckle 2009:36) and Tertia Geldenhuys' sense of distress compels her to call her friends and pastor to pray for them as they feel that the invasion of their farm was due to 'some evil force controlling the people [and] that God alone could save them' (Buckle 2009:32).

Second, following the biblical verse, are 'Eye-witness and News Reports' (Buckle 2009:27) describing the horrific ecological disaster playing itself on the invaded farms. The reports describe, in a raw and spontaneous way (Bolger, Davis and Eshkol 2003:580), how the war veterans had taken over and militarised the area; invaded farmhouses and looted or destroyed furniture and other property such as cars; and let cattle out into confining and distressing spaces. They thus document 'the horror and devastation' (Buckle 2009:37) taking place in the Chinhoyi farming region where Two Tree Hill is located. Buckle represents this context of horror and turmoil in an effort to invoke an apocalyptic image of the land invasions. The invasions turned farms into 'war zones' (Buckle 2009:31) (as Meryl has to enter Two Tree Hill under armed police escort to rescue distressed animals) noted by the remapping of pockets of the farms into war veterans' bases from which they would launch their attacks against 'imperialist' white farmers. Even '[t]he farmhouse had been completely destroyed and was just a blackened empty shell. It had been looted, trashed and then burnt down. Meryl stood staring at the horror and trying to get her emotions under control before she went in' (Buckle 2009:33). Meryl is thus associated with a heroic and messianic aura.

The displacing of the farmers, as in a state of war, meant that the hurried escape left the domestic herds, pets and game abandoned and, hence, at the mercy of the war veterans. The owners of Two Tree Hill, the Geldenhuys family, left behind their cattle herd and were eager to have them and their Australian Cattle Dogs back with them, especially the one dog called Nandi. This highlights the notion about human animal relations, how human and animal lives are intertwined (Huggan and Tiffin 2010; Shikha 2011) and how society has been able to forge that socially equitable and sustainable co-existence with nature and animals throughout time (Vital 2008:87–88). At Two Tree Hill, human and dog relations went beyond the utility value of the Australian Cattle Dog for herding cattle, to the realm of warm human-animal companionship, hence the Geldenhuys' special request for Nandi to be rescued. Furthermore, the dog Nandi became the inspiring symbol of hope for Meryl during the unfolding of this ecological crisis to the extent that Nandi's picture graces the book's cover jacket.

The abandonment of the pets and other animals is depicted as an incomprehensible act. The novel implies the existence of conflicting perceptions about how to relate with animals and the farm landscape by comparing the perceptions of commercial farmers, the landed class, with those of the new settlers seeking to correct historical legacies in a radical way. Here, we are inclined to invoke Huggan and Tiffin's (2010:12) call for the need to examine the significance of the material in examining the competing ideologies on how to relate with animals and the environment.

In *Innocent Victims* Meryl intercedes on behalf of the displaced farmer to rescue and take care of the abandoned cattle, tamed eland called Em, and the beaten and stolen Australian Cattle Dogs, Nandi and her puppies. This act seems minor in comparison to the Zanu-PF's larger project seeking to redress the historical and colonial legacy, the landlessness of the majority of black Zimbabweans. That is why the police and politicians are described in the Geldenhuys' narratives as 'turning a blind eye' to the invasion and pillaging of the farms. Thus, competing ideological and materialist concerns are at play in the disruption of the ideal human-animal relationship that existed on farms such as Two Tree Hill.

The ecocritical perspective demonstrates itself on the conditions witnessed at Two Tree Hill. The author invokes images of incomprehensibility and destabilisation of the way the human-animal relationship and the ecology of the farm are disrupted as the nationalist project seeking to correct past land divisions takes place. This is portrayed as a forced displacement and disruption of the ideal human-animal relationship that is accompanied by cruelty to the animals and the destruction of the property and the farming environment. The text condemns this. Meryl vividly documents with raw emotion the destruction and looting she witnessed at Two Tree Hill, and other farms. Furthermore, her personal witness elicits the reader's empathy to the plight of the animals. In fact, Meryl's emotionally charged and painstaking search for Nandi assists in the construction of a picture of an abandoned farming outpost, which has been ravaged by looting. The search is punctuated by disappointment after realising that Nandi had been beaten and the other puppies snatched by the occupiers. Nandi had nevertheless, escaped to hide somewhere on the farm, traumatised as she was. Meryl's sense of satisfaction is restored gradually. First, there is the chance discovery of the tame eland, Em, though Em was later slaughtered and eaten by the occupiers, thus showing the image of a world turned upside down by inconsiderate war veterans. Later on, Meryl rescues Nandi and her puppy Khanya. Nandi is taken to a veterinary surgery in Chinhoyi, and then reunited with her owners who relocate to South Africa. By continuing her rescue of other animals in the Chinhoyi farming region, Meryl is depicted as bridging the gap between horror and hope. Her work seeks a committed and humanising restoration, with a messianic tone, of the supposed balanced and 'equitable' human-animal relationship. The rescue and restoration of Nandi can, therefore, be considered as emblematic of the transcendence that would restore post-2000 Zimbabwe into a nation that respects the mutual existence amongst peoples as well as between people and animals.

Buckle draws further on Meryl's vivid diary entries of her first-hand witnessing of the specific horror unfolding on the farms. The social and historical specificities of each farm's invasion and the subsequent abandonment of animals are outlined to us through Meryl's diary. For instance, Fynnlands Farm which was invaded in August 2001, where the farmers 'Andy and Elva's house had been completely trashed and personal possessions strewn everywhere' (Buckle 2009:41), brings Meryl and Buckle to an encounter with a long history of a white farmer committed and passionately as well as romantically linked with the farm. Meryl discovers 'three scraps of paper ... old and handwritten in ink' (Buckle 2009:42) containing a poem written in 1927 by an old matriarch of the Fraser family. The poem resonates with the nineteenth-century Romantic poets' love for nature. It celebrates the free spirit, communion with the trees and flowers and exudes an optimistic hope for a continued presence on Fynnlands Farm. Instead, Meryl witnesses a horrific destruction of the farm property on arrival. The sheep were in distress, with two lying in the swimming pool dead and 114 others confined in a small garden to graze. She and her team of other SPCA officers had been called by the Frasers to search for 'a much loved Staffordshire bitch' (Buckle 2009:41) called Maxi who had been abandoned on the farm. Her arrival at this farm brings together the intersection between animal-human relations and farmers' personal histories on the land. A sad tone is invoked as Meryl encounters how the invasions were facilitating the erasure of white farmer family presences and histories on the land. This becomes an exposé of the way the ruling party sought to expunge other histories and replace them with a grand nationalist historical one that excludes others. At the same time; if the visit to Fynnlands enables Meryl to have a glimpse, through the poem of a past pristine farm life which was also characterised by hope for progression to a better future, then the invasions can be inferred as a transportation of this farm, if not the whole Zimbabwe, into a primordial space-time. This is one such instance of the contradictory representations of latent colonial discourses that fail to see the justifiable need for land redistribution, despite the horrific way in which it was being implemented. Maxi is of course rescued after Meryl advertises a reward for her safe return and is reunited with her owners.

Political party contestations are also depicted as contributing another dynamic to the ecological crisis on the farms. The ideological fight between the nationalist and inward looking Zanu-PF and the multiracial and libertarian MDC party leads to the intensely cruel destruction of white commercial farms owned by pro-opposition farmers such as Iain Kay's Chipesa Farm and Roy Bennett's Charleswood Estate. Chipesa Farm was sealed off in March 2002 by war veterans after a series of previous attacks. For example, in 2000, there were violent attacks on Iain Kay because he openly supported the opposition MDC party. In 2001, his son, some neighbours and his farm labourers were held hostage in the farmhouse for a number of days by war veterans and other invaders. That the cordoning off and declaration of the farm as a no-go area is political is especially illustrated in the political songs that were sung by the invaders, as noted in the cited chorus: '*Beat Kay's head so he understands*,' *they chanted, we're tired of you long-noses*,' *they shouted*. The 'ecology of bleakness' on the farm is witnessed by Meryl, when she encounters a deserted farm village and notes that all the farmworkers had been rendered homeless. Furthermore, the Kays' dogs, Boxer, Sasha, Jip and Bonzo and other animals such as pigs and turkeys were abandoned after the cordoning off of the farm. Politics rendered the white farmer, farmworkers, farm pets and other animals, vulnerable. The Kays' pets were later rescued: Boxer and Sasha by Meryl and her SPCA team and Bonzo and Jip by Iain's wife, Kerry, when the Kays were allowed to return and pick up their personal belongings to give way for the new owners. This experience witnessed by Meryl and represented by Buckle in the text under study, highlights the cruel displacing effects of the land invasions on humans and animals. The cruelty was fuelled by the government's political intolerance to dissent, which in a way, raises questions about the land redistribution programme.

Similar politically motivated invasions and intense disruptions of the ecology and victimisation of animals occurred at Roy Bennett's Charleswood Estate. Bennett, just like Kay, was an active MDC member. He was a 2000 parliamentary election candidate. As a result, politics of vengeance and intolerance to opposition by the hegemonic Zanu-PF contributed largely to the ecological crisis at the estate. This crisis is witnessed and diarised by Meryl and represented by Buckle. The invasion of the farm saw the Bennetts relocating to Ruwa, outside the capital city, Harare, and the abandonment of horses, a herd of cattle and farm dogs. Also rendered vulnerable here were the farmworkers, who were under constant surveillance and subjected to frequent attacks by the army and police personnel who were stationed on the estate to instil fear in other commercial farmers and opposition supporters from the Chimanimani constituency. The crisis on Charleswood is described as marked by unimaginably severe abuse of both humans and animals:

> Meryl's involvement had started in April 2003. By then Meryl had been onto hundreds of seized farms, rescued more dogs, cats, pigs, cattle, sheep and horses than she could count and had come face to face with all manner of people undertaking land invasions. Charleswood, however, was going to be different, Meryl knew it and no amount of past experience could have prepared her for these rescues. On this property more abuses

against people and animals had taken place, and for a longer time than on any farm in the country. Here people had been murdered; rape and torture had taken place; and all but a handful of the farm workers had been evicted from the property. Eight hundred cattle were on the farm, several had been axed, others had been slaughtered and the estate was over-run with government supporters, police, soldiers and members of the CIO. (Buckle 2009:311)

Evident in Buckle's description that is punctuated by images of horror, death, displacement and military surveillance, is an underscoring of the dominance of a violent and repressive state intervention programme on the white commercial farm space. The invasion also engenders anxieties as the ecological crisis and violence did not conform to the desire to right past historical injustices about the land and other natural resources that the post-2000 land reform sought to achieve. Meryl journeys to save Bennett's cattle, which had been attacked by axes, abandoned horses and later the dog, Bokkie, which was severely injured by a mob of settlers after saving Moses, the farm security foreman whose house had been set on fire by the mob of invaders and occupiers. The journeys enable us to enter into the 'ecology of repression and severe cruelty' on the farm. It becomes clear that there were larger forces of political brutality and vengeance that were at play in the post-2000 land invasions and this elicits our post-colonial criticism: that of a hegemonic and repressive African elite under the guise of nationalism.

Apart from rescuing the pets and animals belonging to white commercial farmers, Meryl rescued dogs belonging to some war veterans and settlers on the occupied farms, as she did on one of the visits to the heavily militarised Charleswood Estate. Buckle also depicts Meryl's efforts at rescuing some black farmers' or ordinary opposition party supporters' animals abandoned in the wave of politically motivated violence against the opposition party supporters that went hand in hand with the land invasions. Meryl rescued Mr Masikela's chicken abandoned at his house in the working class township of Chiwaridzo in the mining town of Bindura, outside Harare, after he had been hounded out for supporting the MDC. She also worked hard to try and rescue the various trained dogs which were abandoned at Tredar farm when the Chinhoyi region's farm security guards engaged in a politically motivated strike to demand their severance packages. Government had taken over after the white commercial farmers' forced displacement left farm workers with no source of income or pensions. Meryl and other officers moved around providing food and water to the dogs which were abandoned at the different farms in the Chinhoyi region. They translocated some to Tredar farm. The overcrowding in the dog kennels forced Meryl to make a 'decision that the majority of the dogs would have to be euthenased' (Buckle 2009:182). Thus, the text depicts the different ecological crises characterising the post-2000 land invasions and the unsettling conditions faced, as well as decisions that Meryl had to make.

Meryl's SPCA rescue missions in the animal conservancies such as Bubiana near the southern border town of Beitbridge, Save and Chiredzi, reflect another dynamic of the impact of the land invasions and occupations on the human animal relations and ecology of post-2000 Zimbabwe. The levels of poaching rose during the post-2000 land invasions and occupations of farms and conservancies. The resettled or new farmers, as they were termed in state discourses, wreaked havoc on the conservancies, and this is aptly reflected in Meryl's visits to and what she witnessed at the Bubiana Conservancy. Meryl first visited Guy Hilton-Barber's Barberton Ranch, which is part of the Bubiana Conservancy, in December 2000, to deal with the rise in poaching since the advent of land invasions in February 2000. She received Hilton-Barber's 'poaching report which covered the period from May to December 2000 …[and] detailed 84 wild animals, twelve species, which had been found dead in snares on Barberton Ranch' (Buckle 2009:17). She used the report to arrange meetings to discuss conservation issues with local district councils and communities.

Buckle describes the history of Barberton Ranch as the first wildlife conservancy registered in 1991, which thereafter became the home of a number of black rhinos that were relocated from other places where they were under severe threat from poaching. Other animals relocated to Bubiana include elephant, buffalo, sable, eland and zebra. The success of the Bubiana Conservancy is portrayed in the rise in numbers of the different animals by 2000, its provision of jobs to a number of local people, and its financial support to the farmers in the form of hunting and tourism. The neighbouring Mberengwa communal area also benefited from donor funds and proceeds from the tourism and hunting in this conservancy. Buckle outlines the benefits accruing to the neighbouring villages. These included sewing and gardening projects, the improvement of educational, hospital and road infrastructure and the supply of game meat for the locals' consumption. Evident here is a mutually beneficial coexistence between the conservancy holders and neighbouring communities. Thus, the disruption of this successful balance through poaching and the establishment of settlements on the conservancy owing to the land invasions and occupations can only be viewed as a huge threat to the already existing interdependence between man and nature. A puzzling inaction by state institutions such as the police, District Councils and Department of National Parks, is pointed out by Meryl and depicted by Buckle in an effort to underline the tragic aspect of the land invasions. These rising cases of poaching and the paralysis of state departments to do anything about it, reflect the government's complicity in the disruption of thriving conservancy programmes. This elicits criticism.

Meryl's second visit to the conservancy in October 2004 is more tragic and associated with gross apocalyptic imagery. There was a huge increase in the number of animals poached between 2000 and 2004. An environmental apocalypse is reflected in the gross cruelty against animals noted in the way '390 animals [were] found dead in snares and left to rot in the lowveld sun' (Buckle 2009:301). Further ecological horror is documented in the text's reference to Guy Hilton-Barber's report on the way the land invasions impacted severely on the Bubiana Conservancy ecosystem:

> There has been an obvious disappearance of the smaller creatures that constitute the food-chain. Rock rabbits, hares, tortoises, squirrels, mongooses, honey badgers, antbears, otters, waterfowl, guinea fowl, partridges, francolins – list is endless and affects the predators and raptors, etc. No account can be taken of the degree of horror of animal suffering and the enormous wastage of meat. The destruction of the environment, hundreds of thousands of trees being felled and the cultivation of several thousand hectares of land in [a] fragile ecosystem will soon result in a desert. [...] Conservationists watch and weep as 20 years of wildlife resources are decimated within four years. The entire scenario is hugely offensive to any civilised society as the Government's policy of resettling the invaders elsewhere continues in its significant state of political paralysis. (Buckle 2009:301)

Hilton-Barber's comments sum up the epic proportions, in this case tinged with apocalyptic imagery, of environmental destruction that occurred during the land invasions. The comments also highlight the contesting views on how to handle conservancy issues in relation to what might be considered a national developmental project (the Zimbabwe government's land resettlement programme). Hilton-Barber and, by extension, Meryl and Buckle, who are strong animal and environment activists, rightly condemn these adverse effects of the land invasions. All three are critical of the national government for its blanket support for the project for political expedience.

It should be underscored that their criticism of the repressive nature and disregard of the environmental effects associated with the government discourses and implementation of the land invasions is justified. The case, however, extends our understanding of post-colonial ecocriticism in that the Zimbabwe government's notion of development is inward-looking and does not seek to further Western control of the former colonised world's resources. What is clear is that such a condition, where it is the nationalist elite that turn repressive and exclusionary in the face of residual colonialism and contemporary Western imperialist threats, demands complex post-colonial criticism. This Zimbabwean case is indeed paradoxical in that addressing the historical land anomaly was justifiable, but not at the gross expense of the environment, animals and human life on the white commercial farms. Furthermore, the colonial discourses, evident in the way Hilton-Barber and Meryl invoke apocalyptic images and equate the land invasions' adverse impact to the fall from progressive development and civilisation, should be condemned for entrenching the polarities that lead to the divisions affecting the Zimbabwean post-2000 conditions. Nevertheless, it is highly critical as noted by (Shikha 2011) that humanity tries as much as possible to respect its interdependence with nature and act to preserve the surviving flora and fauna for its future survival. As a result, national developmental projects, be they ideologically or historically justified, should consider the diverse histories and economic and environmental concerns, otherwise the nation state, as was witnessed in Zimbabwe, plunges into crisis.

Meryl's Activism and Testing the Zanu-PF Grand Narrative of White Farmer Exclusion

The text's narrative threading of the presence of white farms and the depiction of the white farmer's narrative about their attachment to the farm and ties with the region are an indictment on the Zanu-PF-led nationalist discourse denying white farmers the right to belong and identify with Zimbabwe and its land. Meryl's travels to rescue the stranded animals take us to all corners of the country. Her visits to the invaded farms are a narrative indicator of white presence in Zimbabwe, no matter the historical baggage. As a result, this can be viewed as a narrative metaphor of the way Zimbabwe's history and imaginary of the nation should come to terms with the fact that dotted on its social and geographical mapping of the nation are pockets of white existence. Buckle always includes the story about how particular farmers had been displaced, thus humanising the white farmer and pronouncing their presence and perhaps, their right to the land, albeit under threat from the post-2000 crisis.

The human story of the presence of the white farmer on the Zimbabwean land is juxtaposed with Meryl's documented, personal witnessing of the devastations on the farms and rescue efforts. For instance, Buckle in her description of the presence of the Cartwrights on a Marondera farm, called Waltondale, paints a positive image of Guy and Rosalind Cartwright as committed farmers who also assisted the local community:

> Waltondale had been in the Cartwright family since 1934. It had not been designated by the government for redistribution but was obviously highly sought-after. The farm produced tobacco and maize and had 700 beef cattle. The Cartwrights had built a school on the farm and 400 hundred children were enrolled in Waltondale Farm School. (Buckle 2009:105)

The background story here portrays the Cartwrights as a family with a long and committed connection with land and a family that seeks prosperity and pays back to the community through the school they built on the farm. This human story makes white farmers appear as 'poor' victims of a nationalist project gone wrong. The human story also invokes the reader's empathy, for the farmer is depicted as an ordinary and committed person and hence not the kind of greedy imperialist monster that the Zanu-PF discourses wanted the world to see.

The presence, and hence claim of belonging on the land, is nevertheless portrayed as contradictory. Some whites, such as the Murrays whose August Hill Farm was invaded in August 2003 are portrayed as having historical connections to land. However, the text is able to register the contestations over belonging on and ownership of this land. Buckle clearly shows that although the Murrays bought August Hill Farm in 1968 and struggled for years, beginning in 1974, with the building of the farmhouse, the land was historically occupied by the San hunters, as evidenced by their rock paintings on the farm. It later belonged to the local and nearby black community as attested by a contractor engaged on the farm, Thomas Nyakudya's oral narrative of his ancestors' presence and claim to the farm too. The paradox and contested presence and ownership of land and belonging in former colonised nations are thus portrayed. What is interesting is that the case typically portrays a post-colonial theme of contested histories between the coloniser and the former colonised.

Nevertheless, the ecocritical aspect to be considered here is that if post-colonial ecological criticism seeks a balance and mutual coexistence between men, animals and the environment (Shikha 2011), then the exclusionary and black nationalist Zanu-PF government should have sought a land redistribution programme that strikes a balance between the two contesting ownership narratives. Post-2000 Zimbabwe is thus criticised for failing to strive for an all-inclusive redefinition of the access to land and a sense of national identity, whose impact would not disturb both the environment and human ecology on the farms and throughout the country.

Meryl's rescuing of animals is emblematic of her yearning to assert her sense of belonging and identification with the Zimbabwean nation. The diary, as discussed earlier, is associated with the innermost views and raw emotions about the diarist's encounters (Bolger, Davis and Eshkol 2003; Podnicks 2000). The fact that Meryl's diary predominantly documents her inner views, while rescuing the abandoned animals around Zimbabwe, is reflective of this passionate commitment not only to the welfare of the animals, but also to a crisis-free Zimbabwe. Meryl's heroism, where she rescues all abandoned animals, irrespective of whether they belong to a displaced white commercial farmer, black Zimbabwean commercial or peasant farmer, ordinary citizen, war veteran or new settler on the farm, is implicitly portrayed as the ideal national heroism and commitment as well as citizenry that would restore the early twenty-first century Zimbabwean nation to a healing and ecological balance.

Finally, Meryl's activism, especially the ecological advocacy element, where she fought to improve the plight of abandoned animals and expose the post-2000 ecological crisis unfolding on the various farms and conservancies to the rest of the world, is also significant. The advocacy maps the counter discourses and pro-environmental practices seeking to eradicate the ecologically destructive ones. While the state-sanctioned land invasions were mapped by the state as historically justified, the associated cruelty on the animals and farmers, and the horrible disruption of the farms' ecological balance, can only be viewed as destructive practices deserving condemnation. Meryl's diary entries and their knitting into a literary work by Buckle are thus a counter discourse; they speak back to and against the ecological destruction brought about by land invasions.

In addition, the text was published in England, thus positioning itself for international consumption and, hence a global exposure of the crisis. It calls for global criticism of the adverse effects of the post-2000 Zimbabwe land invasions, farm occupations and fast track land reform programme.

Meryl herself links up with other environmental advocacy groups from countries such as South Africa, Australia and the United Kingdom. She is invited to these countries and given awards for her environmental activism and featured on global media platforms addressing the ecological crisis bedevilling post-2000 Zimbabwe. Such a commitment to save Zimbabwe's animals can, therefore, only be construed as a yearning to assert her commitment for an ecologically balanced, animal friendly nation. It is also an attempt to claim a presence in the nation's trajectories, for Meryl also positions herself as a concerned and committed Zimbabwean white animal activist and citizen.

Conclusion

The chapter's examination of Buckle's representations of Meryl Harrison's animal rights activism during the period between July 2000 and December 2004, underscores the way in which the post-2000 land invasions and farm occupations impacted negatively on human-animal interactions and the ecology of the affected farms. Meryl Harrison's travels around the country to rescue animals are indeed used by the author as a trope to portray large scale horror on the country's invaded and occupied farms, where farm owners were violently displaced, animals left in distress, and houses, cars and other property looted. As a result, it is through Meryl and Buckle's perceptions and representations that the ecological horrors on the farms are portrayed vividly for us to view and condemn. The representations also enable us to note the ideological and ecological contestations characterising the post-colonial condition of a post-2000 Zimbabwe.

Therefore, Meryl's experiences depict the competing ideologies on how to interact with land, nature and animals in times of crisis, and how we can best re-map ownership patterns over national resources. It is clear that these contestations playing themselves out on the site of the white-owned farms, disrupt notions on belonging and citizenship, and ultimately emblematise the contradictions associated with the post-colonial trajectories of Zimbabwe since 2000. Nevertheless, the Zimbabwean white farmers, such as Iain Kay and Roy Bennett, and environmental activists such as Meryl and by extension Buckle, claim to be Zimbabweans or still identify and seek to belong and be considered Zimbabwean. The claim for inclusion is significant, for it speaks to the need for a comprehensive imaginary of what it is to be Zimbabwean and how a healthy nation can be restored, as suggested by the positive effects of Meryl's work where a number domestic farm animals and wild animals are rescued and reunited with their owners, and those cruelly beaten or violated are healed and restored.

8

White Belonging and Identity in Zimbabwe in the Twenty-first Century

It is evident in this study that land is very central in post-colonial Zimbabwe's social and political imaginary. The various inter-textual references to the political rhetoric produced by the Zanu-PF politicians in the electronic and print media, especially noted in Buckle's (2000 and 2003) memoirs, and repeated in the war veterans' political discourse about how the white Rhodesians came from Europe and stole the land from black Zimbabweans represented in most of the literary works on the post-2000 land invasions, attest to this significance. In addition, the dominance of the politics about land and its role in the formation of contesting narratives about land are a major theme in the literary history of representations focusing on land in post-colonial Zimbabwe. This is noted in the critical studies that examine the fictional representations of experiences, perceptions and contestations for land in Zimbabwe at various stages in the historical trajectories of the country.

The social and political imaginings vary in accordance with how land has been perceived, defined and used, and by whom, throughout the different stages in Zimbabwe's colonial and post-colonial history (Nyamunda 2014). The African perception on the land during the pre-colonial and early colonial period was, as noted by Ranger (1999b), characterised by a combination of a spiritual and sustainable use of the land. This contrasted with the early Rhodesian settler spatial divisions that were built on imperialist notions that valued the use of scientific agricultural methods and stereotypically labelled the indigenous people as primitive and indifferent to the environment. Up to the 1950s, this conflicting perception of land and the environment led to the violent displacement of the indigenous peoples from their ancestral lands. Such displacements created a cultural and historical rift between whites and blacks, the landed and the dispossessed, the coloniser and the colonised and other Manichean divisions that continued to be reproduced in the different social and spatial definitions existing in colonial and post-independent Zimbabwe. The post-2000 land invasions and fast track land reform programme are therefore a result of the long history of contestations over the nation's social and political imaginary of land and belonging.

In fact, the land invasions, especially the accompanying displacement of the white commercial farmers and land-owning black Zimbabweans who opposed the ruling Zanu-PF party's fast track land reform programme, are brought to the fore in discourses on national connectedness and belonging. As has been noted in the previous chapters, especially Chapter 3 where Buckle's memoirs are discussed, the accompanying grand narrative about the land invasions, occupations and fast track land reform, labelled white farmers as outsiders, remnants of Rhodesian colonialism and Europeans not deserving any connection with the historically 'black' nation. As a result, as documented in Rogers' (2009) memoir and Meryl's diary (Buckle 2009), discussed in Chapters 6 and 7 respectively, whites were displaced from their farms to places of refuge mainly in the Zimbabwean cities. Some were ultimately forced to translocate to regional countries such as South Africa or international destinations such as the United Kingdom, Australia and New Zealand. Even Meryl, the chief protagonist and diarist from whom the text under discussion in Chapter 7 draws its narrative, migrated to the UK after being fired by the SPCA. The nexus between displacement and intra-and-international migration reflects how the land invasions and the land reform programme indeed redefined notions of national identities and belonging in Zimbabwe. Nevertheless, some whites, as the Bourke family does in Lang's *Place of Birth* (2006) discussed in Chapter 4, claim belonging and pronounce their white 'Zimbabweaness', just as Buckle's (2009) literary diary, discussed in Chapter 7, describes Meryl's experiences during the first four years of the post-2000 Zimbabwean crisis.

It should be noted that the post-2000 tumultuous experiences led to the production of a number of white narratives about land in Zimbabwe. Memoirs, journalistic and fictional narratives representing white farmers' experiences and imaginings on the land invasions, farm occupations and the government's fast track land redistribution programme indeed came into prominence during the period 2000 to 2010. The texts vary in their portrayal of the contestations over the land, the nature of the land invasions and their impact on the domestic spaces and memories of the affected protagonists. They describe the new mappings and perceptions that were constituted during this epoch and its overall re-definition of Zimbabwe's post-colonial condition in the twenty-first century. They portray further, the way white commercial farmers and writers claim belonging and hence Zimbabwean citizenship. However, as noted in Lamb's (2006) text, where Nigel is, by the end of the text, making interracial connections with Aqui and opposition MDC black Zimbabweans, a better Zimbabwe can only be constituted from these radical cross-overs between races. Perhaps, people like Nigel had to accept the country's historical burden about land and find compromises, uncomfortable as they maybe, to recognise the multiple perceptions about and claims to land.

Buckle's memoirs, *African Tears* and *Beyond Tears*, are significant in that they illustrate Zimbabwe's place in the larger global politics and thus call for a national imaginary that takes into consideration this geopolitics, no matter how uncomfortable that might be. First, Buckle's texts expand Zimbabwe's representation of the post-2000 land invasions into the larger globalised space of wider circulation and consumption. This can be viewed as a meta-narrative signifying the new imaginary trends, where the local and the global are easily linked and any experience is easily disseminated to the world. This means that any retrogressive action, such as the way the historically legitimate need for land redistribution was distorted owing to the war veterans' violent and destructive invasions, is easily accessed all over the world and will elicit global reaction. Therefore, Buckle's memoirs seem to be suggesting the need for Zimbabwe to find a solution to the land issue that incorporates the country's multiple perspectives on the land and belonging as well as the current global social and economic factors that also impact on this twenty-first century trajectories.

Furthermore, while specific historical experiences and conditions determine the way national and other identities are constituted, the global perspective has to be considered as it is rising prominently to be another determining factor in the definition and re-imagining of one's sense of the self. While one might argue that the task of post-colonial students is to resist the domination of global political thoughts and consumption patterns, which usually reflect the Euro-American social, economic and political interests, one must also acknowledge that the same new media technologies also reach a readership consisting of victims of the same major global powers' social and cultural domination. Victims and agents of change are thus likely to offer their solidarity and voices of resistance. Buckle's memoirs, just as her literary diary of Meryl's experiences as she saves animals which were abandoned during the invasions, also portray the rise of a literary trend focusing on advocacy and human rights narration in contemporary Zimbabwean literary production.

Lang's *Place of Birth*, suggests the need for subversion of a grand narrative about history and belonging to the land. The novel describes the Bourke siblings' recollection of their childhood experiences on the farm. Their particular individualities and colonial Rhodesian personhood are indeed constituted from their connections with the farm's landscape and connections with other white farmers' families in the Shangani area.

They have a long family history on the farm dating back to their great-grandfather's establishment of the farm during the early pioneer settlers' era and their grandparents and parents' work to establish a home and sustainable farm, is portrayed as central in establishing intimate and justifiable links to the land. Such personal histories are portrayed by Lang as subverting the grand nationalist narrative of the land that Zanu-PF is propagating, where whites are defined as foreigners with no spiritual links to the land in Zimbabwe. Nevertheless, the siblings are displaced and rendered restless, owing to the state's violent erasure of their own history and spiritual linkage to Hopelands Farm. As a result, one way of undermining the negative impact of the post-2000 exclusionary discourses is to allow the inscription of histories and memories other than those presented by the government in the redefinition of identities that the post-2000 land invasions envision.

Lang in *Place of Birth*, just as Lamb does in *House of Stone*, also notes that while the redefinition of connections to the nation and access to the land is inevitable and justified, the violence and chaos accompanying the project, should not be tolerated. The invasions seem to be offering the possibility for both white and black Zimbabweans to re-evaluate their perceptions of the land and notions of belonging. In fact, the other texts expand Lang's suggestion by reflecting that the solution to achieving non-violent ways of relating as a nation and accessing as well as belonging to the land can be through the establishment of social relations through discussions (Aqui and Nigel in Lamb's *House of Stone*) or strategic relationships (Lyn Rogers and Tendai as well as Lyn and Walter in *The Last Resort*) between the different Zimbabwean races and classes.

Finally, it should be noted that these white narratives have also encouraged the growth of more literature that is based on or recognises the existence of the post-2000 land issue. The fact that the control of historical memory and narrative is central in the re-imagining of the land in the post-2000 era, has led to the birth of texts written by white Zimbabweans that re-read the nation's history, reimagine the role of the Zanu-PF leadership, especially its leader Robert Mugabe in relation to the land invasions, and others that assess the impact of the land invasions and the fast track land reform programme on the black farmers who benefited from the land reform programme.

First, Geoff Hill's *Battle for Zimbabwe: The Final Countdown* (2003) reviews the nation's history. Hill's narrative style starts from the present, where he presents the South African setting and experiences of some ordinary Zimbabweans in exile after their displacement because of the post-2000 crisis in Zimbabwe. He then shifts his narrative's spatial and time setting into Zimbabwe and then back to South Africa while focussing on immediate past experiences associated with post-2000 land invasions, and the country's major historical events that include 1890s British and then BSAC's colonial intrusion and conquest of Mashonaland and Matabeleland, Rhodesian colonialism, the 1970s black nationalist's anti-colonial war and the 1980s reconciliation and development era. Hill's intertextual references to history are subversive in that they depict his narrative affirmation of the country's 'real' past history that undermines the state-controlled one, dubbed patriotic history by Ranger (2005) seeking to dominate the nation's social and historical imaginary.

Second, Heidi Holland in *Dinner with Mugabe: The Untold Story of a Freedom Fighter Who Became a Tyrant* (2008) uses the biographical narrative to delve into Mugabe's personal history from a point informed by her observation of the social, political and economic crisis crippling Zimbabwe, which was among other factors, triggered by the land invasions. Holland's biography portrays a new trend in white narratives, which moves from addressing white experiences and victimhood, as done by writers such as Buckle, to an attempt at understanding the experiences of blacks during the invasions. Holland's book indeed unpacks Mugabe's personal experiences and psyche in relation to the African nationalist struggle, personal tragedies and issue such as the British New Labour Party and Clare Short's public diplomacy in which, according to Mugabe and his close confidantes such as the Catholic figure, Father Mukonori, the British reneged on promises to fund land reform as per previous agreements with the Conservative Party-led government and the earlier 1979 Lancaster House Conference promises, hence the post-2000 land invasions and the associated tumult within the white and black Zimbabwean community.

Third, Pilosoff's *Unbearable Whiteness of Being: Farmers' Voices from Zimbabwe* (2012), a historical analysis of white discourses available in the *Farmer Magazine* and other archives cited in this book, adds to this body of work by white writers examining the white farmers' experiences and how they connect with land and nation during the colonial, post-independence and especially post-2000 period in Zimbabwe.

Finally, Hanlon, Manjengwa and Smart (all white writers as Manjengwa is a white writer and academic married to a black Zimbabwean military officer) in their text, *Zimbabwe Takes Back its Land* (2013), which is written from an environmental and development studies point of view, draws on the Zanu-PF grand narrative about land to outline the growth of production by the new black farmers and beneficiaries of the fast track land reform programme in Zimbabwe's Mashonaland East and Central provinces. Hanlon, Manjengwa and Smart provide a new angle at perceiving the land issue in Zimbabwe, in that they are a set of white academic authors who have shifted the focus from white farmers' experiences to the black farmers' experiences. Their analytical strand has been the subject of intense criticism from various scholars such as Nyamunda (2014) and Pilossof (2014), owing to the authors' use of a problematic and anecdotal methodology and their failure to engage with critical literature on land in Zimbabwe. Nevertheless, the focus on connectedness to the land and how it is imagined as well as remembered in Zimbabwe, is still subject to continued contestations as aptly noted in the different angles of perceptions and thematic focuses in the texts discussed as well as the way texts such as Hanlon, Manjengwa and Smart's (2013) opened up critical historical debate on the impact of the post-2000 fast track land reform programme.

There are other literary strands that focus on the land invasions' effect on the lives of whites and other citizens in the city that I have not examined but which point to the continued focus on this subject in the Zimbabwean literary imaginary. Godwin's *When a Crocodile Eats the Sun* (2006) is a typical example of a text, written in a memoir style, which shows the intricate links between land invasions and the social and economic dislocation suffered by some commercial farmers, his parents and the other urban white and black characters in Harare and other cities in Zimbabwe. The text is mostly about Godwin's experiences with his parents while he is visiting his dying father and 'about his own identity issues, starting with his discovery that his father was a Polish Jew who lost his family in the holocaust' (Kriger 2008:161). However, these experiences are closely linked with the negative social, economic and political effects of the land invasions that have come to destabilise the routine of his parents' lives and that of other urban residents in Harare. His father, a retired civil servant and his mother, a dedicated medical doctor at the disintegrating referral Parirenyatwa Hospital in Harare, are described, just as other urban Zimbabweans, as suffering from incessant shortages of basic foodstuffs, water, electricity and even cash. At the same time, Godwin's journalistic assignments for the foreign newspapers that he writes for as a freelance correspondent, take him to various commercial farming districts, such as Centenary. It is on such assignments that the text links the main plot, which is about Godwin's journey depicting his own struggle to come to terms with his Jewish identity, and the tragic events happening on the invaded farms. The domestic and the urban experiential spaces, as illustrated in the Godwin's' experiences in Harare, and the public and commercial farm ones are structurally linked in this memoir. This, therefore, shows that some of the white Zimbabweans' post-2000 literary productions are still preoccupied with the impact of the post-2000 land invasions, but nevertheless they are expanding their imaginings to incorporate the invasions' effects on the larger urban spaces and the country's larger social, political and economic sectors.

Finally, there is evidence of a production of new fiction that describes the land invasions, but is written in other genres, other than the non-fictive memoirs dominating this study. Pauline Henson's *Countdown* (2008) is a political detective novel that describes the difficulties encountered by policemen as they investigate crimes on farms in 2002. There is also Sean Christie's travel story 'I had a farm in Africa' (2008) published in the *Mail & Guardian*, South Africa, which describes the writers' 60 kilometre bicycle journey from Harare to a Norton farm that used to belong to his grandfather. The usual themes of restlessness and dislocation are treated, as noted in Christie's fears for his life, should he be captured by the new owner of the farm, and his anger after noticing that the new owner has destroyed the farm and farmhouse which hold nostalgic memories for him. He is also disillusioned with the land reform programme after uniting with some of his grandfather's old farmworkers who have been reduced to poverty as they are unemployed and without any hope for a better future.

That the land invasions and government's land redistribution project will continue to act as a prompt for most post-2000 literary productions, especially those from white Zimbabweans, is confirmed by these and other new recent writings that might have been overlooked here. However, what is intriguing about these new and old productions is that apart from describing the violent and chaotic nature of and other social and ideological contestations over the land, they also depict a yearning for new ways of looking at the land invasions. These new ways include calls for the recognition of heterogeneous perceptions of land and narratives about history, as for instance, highlighted by Lamb (2006). Furthermore, there is a need to embrace pragmatism in the attempts at redefining what it means to be Zimbabwean and who qualifies to call themselves Zimbabwean. More importantly, as indicated by various literary works, studied in detail here, and in the new genres reflected in the recent creative imaginings on the land, there is a need for readers and the protagonists occupying the represented worlds to widen their thoughts as they try to unpack the complexities characterising the post-2000 land invasions, no matter how discomforting they may be – something that academic studies such as Hanlon, Manjengwa and Smart's (2012) text has begun, although the text has its weaknesses as noted by reviewers such as Nyamunda (2014) and Pilossof (2014).

References

Achebe, C. 1960. *Things Fall Apart*. London: Heinemann.

Aijimer, G. and Abbink, J. (eds). 2000. *Meanings of Violence: A Cross Cultural Perspective*. Oxford: Berg.

Alexander, A. 2007. 'The Historiography of Land in Zimbabwe: Strengths, Silences and Questions', *Safundi: The Journal of South African and American Studies*, 8(2):183–198.

Alexander, J., McGregor, J. and Ranger, T. 2000. *Violence and Memory: One Hundred Years in the 'Dark Forests' of Matabeleland*. London: James Currey.

Anderson, B. 1986. *Imagined Communities: Reflections on the Origins and Spread of Nationalism*. London: Verso.

Ashcroft, B. 1994. 'Excess: Post-colonialism and the Verandas of Meanings', in Tiffin, C. and Lawson, A. (eds), *De-scribing Empire: Postcolonialism and Textuality*. London and New York: Routledge, 33–34.

Ashcroft, B., Griffiths, G. and Tiffin, H. (eds). 1995. *The Post-Colonial Studies Reader*. London: Routledge.

Ballinger, W. 1966. *Call it Rhodesia*. London: Mayflower.

Bauer, J.J. and McAdams, D.P. 2004. '"Personal Growth in Adults" Stories of Life Transitions'. *Journal of Personality*, 72(3):573–602.

Blok, A. 2000. 'The Enigma of Senseless Violence', in Aijimer, G. and Abbink, J. (eds) *Meanings of Violence: A Cross Cultural Perspective*. Oxford and New York: Berg, 1–22.

Bolger, N., Davis A. and Eshkol, R. 2003. 'Diary Methods: Capturing Life as Lived', in *Annual Review of Psychology*, 54:579–616.

Bower, C. 2006. 'They had the Experience…but missed the Meaning'. Book Review of *House of Stone* by Christina Lamb. Available on: http://www. newenglishreview.org/custpage.cfm?frm=3343&sec_id=3343. Accessed on 6 November 2008.

Brenner, R.F. 2003. *Writing as Resistance: Four Women Confronting the Holocaust.* University Park: Penn State University Press.

Brubaker, R. and Cooper, F. 2000. 'Beyond "Identity"', *Theory and Society,* 29:1–47.

Buckle, C. 2000. *African Tears: The Zimbabwean Land Invasions.* Cape Town: Jonathan Ball.

Buckle, C. 2003. *Beyond Tears: Zimbabwe's Tragedy.* Cape Town: Jonathan Ball.

Buckle, C. 2009. *Innocent Victims: Rescuing the Stranded Animals of Zimbabwe's Farm Invasions – Meryl Harrison's Extraordinary Story.* London: Merlin Unwin.

Bunn, D. 1996. 'Comparative Barbarism: Game Reserves, Sugar Plantations, and the Modernization of South African Landscape', in Darian-Smith, K., Gunner, L. and Nuttall, S. (eds), *Text, Theory, Space: Land, Literature and History in South Africa and Australia.* London and New York: Routledge. 37–52.

Carter, P. 1987. *The Road to Botany: An Essay in Spatial History.* London: Faber and Faber.

Chinx, C. 2001. *Hondo Yeminda Vol 1 & 2.* Harare: Zimbabwe Music Corporation.

Chan, S. and Primorac, R. 2004. 'The Imagination of Land and the Reality of Seizure: Zimbabwe's Complex Reinventions', *Journal of International Affairs,* 57(2):63–80.

Chennells, A. 1982. 'Settler Myths and the Southern Rhodesian Novel.' PhD Thesis, University of Zimbabwe.

Chennells, A. 1991. 'Cultural Violence during the Pax Rhodesiana: The Evidence from Rhodesian Fiction', International Conference on Political Violence in Southern Africa'. Oxford: St Anthony's College. June 25–27.

Chennells, A. 1995. 'Rhodesian Discourse, Rhodesian Novels and the Zimbabwe Liberation War' in Bhebhe, N. and Ranger, T. (eds), *Society in Zimbabwe's Liberation War.* Harare: University of Zimbabwe Publications. 102–129.

Chennells, A. 1999. 'Essential Diversity: Post-colonial Theory and African Literature', *Brno Studies in English,* 25:109–126.

Chikwava, B. 2009. *Harare North*. London: Jonathan Cape.

Christie, S. 2008. 'I had a farm in Africa', *Mail & Guardian*. Available on: http://mg.co.za/article/2008-12-22-i-had-a-farm-in-africa-young-mans-journey. Accessed on 12 February 2009.

Chuma, W. 2004. 'Liberating or Limiting the Public Sphere? Media Policy and the Zimbabwe Transition, 1980-2004' in Raftopoulos, B. and Savage, T. (eds), *Zimbabwe: Injustice and Political Reconciliation*. Cape Town: Institute for Justice and Reconciliation, 119–139.

Commercial Farmers Union Report. 2011. Zimbabwe Environmental and Wildlife Catastrophe – Conservancies. Mike Campbell Foundation. 20 October. Available on http://www.mikecampbellfoundation.com/page/environmental-crisis-conservancies-report. Accessed on 22 September 2013.

Conrad. J. [1899] 1982. *Heart of Darkness*. Hammondsworth: Penguin.

Darian-Smith, K., Gunner, L. and Nuttall, S. (eds). 1996. 'Introduction', in: Darian-Smith, K. Gunner, L. and Nuttall, S. (eds), *Text, Theory, Space: Land, Literature and History in South Africa and Australia*. London and New York: Routledge. 1–20.

Fanon, F. 1963. *The Wretched of the Earth*. London: Penguin.

Freeman, L. 2005. 'Contradictory constructions of the Crisis in Zimbabwe', *Historia*, 50(2):287–310.

Fuller, A. 2003. *Don't Let's Go to the Dogs Tonight*. London: Picador.

Gappah, P. 2009. *An Elegy of Easterly*. London: Faber and Faber.

Godwin, P. 1996. *Mukiwa: A white Boy in Africa*. London: Picador.

Godwin, P. 2006. *When a Crocodile Eats the Sun*. Cape Town: Pan Macmillan.

Groenewald, Y. 2002a. 'Zimbabwe Land Reform Decimates Game', *Mail & Guardian,* 16–22 August.

Groenewald, Y. 2002b. 'Rhinos Fall Victims to Zim Chaos', *Mail & Guardian,* 30 August–5 September.

Groenewald, Y. 2003. 'Zim Wild Life Pillage Continues', *Mail & Guardian* 8–14 August.

Haggard, R.H. 1955. *King Solomon's Mines*. London: Collins.

Hammar, A. and Raftopoulos, B. 2003. 'Zimbabwe's Unfinished Business: Rethinking Land, State and Nation' in Hammar A, Raftopoulos, B. and Jensen, S. (eds), *Zimbabwe's Unfinished Business: Rethinking Land, State and Nation in the Context of Crisis*. Harare: Weaver Press, 1–47.

Hancock, I. and Godwin, P. 1993. *'Rhodesians Never Die': The Impact of War and Political Change on White Rhodesians c.1970-1980*. Oxford: Oxford University Press.

Hanlon, J., Manjengwa, J. and Smart, T. 2013. *Zimbabwe Takes Back its Land*. Sunnyside: Jacana.

Harris, A. 2005. 'Writing Home: Inscriptions of Whiteness/Descriptions of Belonging in White Zimbabwean Memoir-autobiography', in Muponde, R. and Primorac, R. (eds), *Versions of Zimbabwe: New Approaches to Literature and Culture*. Harare: Weaver Press, 103–117.

Hartnack, A. 2014. 'Whiteness and Shades of Grey: Erasure, Amnesia and the Ethnography of Zimbabwe's Whites', *Journal of Contemporary African Studies*, DOI: 10.1080/02589001.2013.873590

Henson, P. 2008. *Countdown*. Cape Town: Jonathan Ball

Hill, G. 2003. *The Battle for Zimbabwe: The Final Countdown*. Cape Town: Zebra Press.

Hoba, L. 2009. *The Trek and Other Stories*. Harare: Weaver Press.

Holding, I. 2005. *Unfeeling*. London: Simon & Schuster.

Holland, H. 2008. *Dinner with Mugabe: The Untold Story of a Freedom Fighter Who Became a Tyrant*. Johannesburg: Penguin.

Huggan, G. and Tiffin, H. 2010. *Postcolonial Ecocriticism: Literature, Animals, Environment.* London and New York: Routledge and Taylor & Francis.

Hughes, D.M. 2010. *Whiteness in Zimbabwe: Race, Landscape, and the Problem of Belonging*. New York: Palgrave Macmillan.

Inglis, G. 2000. 'Truth and Fiction: Review Article', *Newfoundland Studies*, 16(1): 67–77.

Jolly, M. 2011. 'Consenting Voices? Activist Life Stories and Complex Dissent'. *Life Writing*, 8(4): 363–374.

Kalaora, L. 2011. 'Madness, Corruption and Exile: On Zimbabwe's Remaining White Commercial Farmers', *Journal of Southern African Studies*, 37(4):747–762.

Kriger, N. 2008. 'Zimbabwe through Multiple Perspectives', *African Studies Review*, 51(3):159–164.

Lamb, C. 2006. *House of Stone: The True Story of a Family Divided in War-Torn Zimbabwe*. London: Random House.

Lang, G. 2006. *Place of Birth*. Cape Town: Jonathan Ball.

Loomba, A. 2005. *Colonialism/Postcolonialism*. London and New York: Routledge.

Mackenzie, J.M. 1988. *The Empire of Nature: Hunting, Conversation and British Imperialism*. Manchester: Manchester University Press.

Macgregor, K. 2006. 'Artist and author Graham Lang may have settled in Australia, but he still grapples with his intense yearning for Africa', *The Witness*, 1 July.

Makunike, C. 2008. Christina Lamb 'Explains' Africa to her British readers'. Available on https://zimreview.wordpress.com/2008/03/23/christina-lamb-explains-africa-to-her-british-readers/ Accessed on 28 October 2008.

Manase, I. 2011. 'Imagining Post-2000 Zimbabwean Perceptions of Land and Notions on Identities in Catherine Buckle's African Tears: The Zimbabwe Land Invasions', *Journal of Literary Studies*, 27(2):27–36.

Marechera, D. 1978. *House of Hunger*. Oxford: Heinemann.

Maughan-Brown, D. 1985. *Land, Freedom and Fiction*. London: Zed Books.

McAdams, D.P. 2008. 'Personal Narratives and the Life Story', in Oliver P. J., Robins, R.W. and Pervin, L.A. (eds), *Handbook of Personality: Theory and Research*. Third Edition. New York: Guilford Press, 242–262.

McCooey, D. 2004. 'Editorial: Life Writing and the Public Sphere', *Life Writing*, 1(2): vii–xi.

McNeill, L. 2005. 'Editorial: Labelling Ourselves: Genres and Life Writing', *Life Writing*, 1(2):1–18.

Mitchell, W.J.T. (ed.). 1994. *Landscape and Power*. Chicago and London: Chicago University Press.

Moyo, S. 2001. 'The Land Occupation Movement and Democratisation in Zimbabwe: Contradictions of Neoliberalism', *Millennium: Journal of International Studies*, 30(2): 311–330.

Moyo, S. 2005. 'The Land Question and the Peasantry in Southern Africa', Enlibro: Politics and Social Movements in a Hegemonic World: Lessons, from Africa, Asia and Latin America. *Latin American Social Sciences: Buenos Aires*, 275–307.

Mtizira-Nondo, N. 2008. *The Chimurenga Protocol*. Harare: Botshelo.

Mungoshi, C. 1975. *Waiting for the Rain*. London: Heinemann.

Muponde, R. 2004. 'The Worm and the Hoe: Cultural Politics and Reconciliation after the Third Chimurenga' in Raftopoulos, B. and Savage, T. (eds), *Zimbabwe Injustice and Political Reconciliation*. Cape Town: Institute for Justice and Reconciliation, 176–192.

Muponde, R. and Primorac, R. 2005. 'Introduction' in Muponde, R. and Primorac, R. (eds), *Versions of Zimbabwe: New approaches to literature and culture*. Harare: Weaver Press. xiii–xxii.

Noyes, J. 1992. *Colonial Space*. Chur: Harwood Academic.

Nyambi, O. 2013. 'Nation in Crisis: Alternative Literary Representations of Zimbabwe Post-2000'. Unpublished PhD thesis, Stellenbosch University, South Africa.

Nyamunda, T. 2014. 'Insights into Independent Zimbabwe: Some Historiographical Reflections', *Strategic Review for Southern Africa*, 36(1):72–89.

Palmer, R. 1977. *Land and Racial Domination in Rhodesia*. London: Heinemann.

Phimister, I. 2004. 'South African Diplomacy and the Crisis in Zimbabwe; Liberation Solidarity in the 21st Century' in Raftopoulos, B. and Savage, T. (eds), *Zimbabwe Injustice and Political Reconciliation*. Cape Town: Institute for Justice and Reconciliation, 271–291.

Phimister, I. 2005. '*Rambai Makashinga* [Continue to Endure]: Zimbabwe's Unending Crisis'. *Southern African Historical Journal*, 54(1):112–126.

Pilossof, R. 2008. 'The Land Question (Un)Resolved: An Essay Review', *Historia*, 53(2):270–279.

Pilossof, R. 2009. 'The Unbearable Whiteness of Being: Land, Race and Belonging in the Memoirs of White Zimbabweans', *South African Historical Journal*, 61(3):621–638.

Pilossof, R. 2012. *The Unbearable Whiteness of Being: Farmers' Voices from Zimbabwe*. Claremont: UCT Press.

Pilossof, R. 2014. 'Reinventing Significance: Reflections on Recent Whiteness Studies in Zimbabwe (Review article)', *Africa Spectrum*, 3:135–148.

Podnicks, E. 2000. *Daily Modernism: The Literary Diaries of Virginia Woolf, Antonia White, Elizabeth Smart, and Anais Nin*. Quebec: McGill-Queens University Press.

Pongweni, J.C. 1982. *Songs that Won the Liberation War*. Harare: College Press.

Primorac, R. 2006. *The Place of Tears: The Novel and Politics in Modern Zimbabwe*. London & New York: Tauris Academic Studies.

Primorac, R. 2007. 'The Poetics of State Terror in Twenty-First Century Zimbabwe'. *Interventions*, 9 (3):434–450.

Raftopoulos, B. 2003. 'The State in Crisis Authoritarian Nationalism, Selective Citizenship and Distortions of Democracy in Zimbabwe', in Hammar A., Raftopoulos, B. and Jensen, S. (eds), *Zimbabwe's Unfinished Business: Rethinking Land, State and Nation in the Context of Crisis*. Harare: Weaver Press, 217–242.

Raftopoulos, B. 2004. 'Nation Race and History in Zimbabwean Politics', in Raftopoulos, B. and Savage, T. (eds), *Zimbabwe: Injustice and Political Reconciliation*. Cape Town: Institute for Justice and Reconciliation, 160–175.

Raftopoulos, B. and Savage, T. (eds). 2004. *Zimbabwe: Injustice and Political Reconciliation*. Cape Town: Institute for Justice and Reconciliation.

Ranger, T. 1999a. 'African Views of the Land: A Research Agenda', *Transformation: Critical Perspective on Southern Africa*, 44:53–62.

Ranger, T. 1999b. *Voices from the Rocks: Nature, culture and History in the Matopos Hills of Zimbabwe*. Harare: Baobab, Bloomington and Indianapolis: Indiana University Press.

Ranger, T. 2000. 'African Views of the Land: A Research Agenda', *Transformation: Critical Perspective on Southern Africa*, 44:53–62.

Ranger, T. 2005. 'Rule by Historiography: The Struggle over the Past in Contemporary Zimbabwe', in Muponde, R. and Primorac, R. (eds), *Versions of Zimbabwe: New Approaches to Literature and Culture*. Harare: Weaver Press, 217–243.

Rogers, D. 2009. *The Last Resort: A Memoir of Zimbabwe*. Jeppestown: Jonathan Ball.

Roy, A. 1999. 'The Greater Common Good'. Available on http://www.narmada.org/gcg/gcg.html. Accessed on 24 May 2013.

Rutherford, B. 2003. 'Belonging to the Farm(er): Farm Workers, Farmers, and the Shifting Politics of Citizenship', in Hammar, A., Raftopoulos, B. and Jensen, S. (eds), *Zimbabwe's Unfinished Business: Rethinking Land, State and Nation in the Context of Crisis*. Harare: Weaver Press, 191–216.

Shikha, K. 2011. 'Ecocriticism in Indian Fiction'. *IRWLE* 7(1):1–11.

Singer, J.A. 2004. 'Narrative Identity and Meaning Making Across the Adult Lifespan: An Introduction'. *Journal of Personality*, 72(3):437–459.

Spivak, G.C. 1995. 'Can the Subaltern Speak?', in Ashcroft, B., Griffiths, G. and Tiffin, H. (eds), *The Post-Colonial Studies Reader*. London and New York: Routledge, 24–28.

Stroinska, M. and Cecchetto, V. 2015. 'Is Autobiographical Writing a Historical Document?: The Impact of Self-censorship on Life Narratives', *Life Narratives*, 12(2):177–188.

Tagwira, V. 2007. *The Uncertainty of Hope*. Johannesburg: Jacana.

Thram, D. 2006. 'Patriotic History and the Politicisation of Memory: Manipulation of Popular Music to Re-invent the Liberation Struggle in Zimbabwe'. *Critical Arts,* 20(2):75–88.

Veit-Wild, F. 1993. *Teachers, Preachers and Non-Believers: The Social History of Zimbabwean Literature.* Harare: Baobab.

Vital, A. 2008. 'Toward an African Ecocriticism: Postcolonialism, Ecology and *Life & Times of Michael K*', *Research in African Literatures*, 39(1): 87–106.

Walker, C. 2008. *Land-Marked: Land Claims and Land Restitution in South Africa*. Johannesburg: Jacana.

White, G. 2003. *Battle for Zimbabwe: The Final Countdown*. Johannesburg: Struck Press.

Willems, W. 2004a. 'Peasant Demonstrators, Violent Invaders: Representations of Land in the Zimbabwe Press', *World Development*, 32(10):1767–1783.

Willems, W. 2004b. 'Selection and Silence: Contesting Meanings of Land in Zimbabwe', *Ecquid Novi: African Journalism Studies*, 25(1):4–24.

Willems, W. 2005. 'Remnants of Empire? British Media Reporting on Zimbabwe', *Westminster Papers in Communication and Culture*, November: 91–108.

Zimunya, M. 1982. *Those Years of Drought and Hunger: The birth of African Fiction in English*. Gweru: Mambo Press.

Index